CW01559140

Spencer Tracy and Katharine Hepburn: Hollywood's Most Famous Couple

By Charles River Editors

About Charles River Editors

Charles River Editors was founded by Harvard and MIT alumni to provide superior editing and original writing services, with the expertise to create digital content for publishers across a vast range of subject matter. In addition to providing original digital content for third party publishers, Charles River Editors republishes civilization's greatest literary works, bringing them to a new generation via ebooks.

Introduction

Tracy in *Fury* (1936)

Spencer Tracy (1900-1967)

"Know your lines and don't bump into the furniture." – Spencer Tracy

Of all the screen legends whose names remain synonymous with Hollywood, few took as long to become a star as Spencer Tracy, who is today recognized as one of the greatest actors ever but whose career did not truly take off until he was already in his mid-30s. After languishing with Fox for 5 years and over two dozen movies, one biographer had summed up his career to that point in time: "Tracy was scarcely a blip on the box office barometer in 1935, a critics' darling and little more."

However, after joining MGM in 1935, Tracy catapulted to fame with one of the most impressive runs in Hollywood history, winning Oscars for Best Actor in 1938 and 1939 after already being nominated in 1937. Over the next three decades, Tracy would appear in classics like *Captains Courageous* and *Judgment at Nuremburg*, appear in 9 films with Katharine Hepburn, and receive 9 Oscar nominations over a span of 32 years, including for his final film, *Guess Who's Coming to Dinner*. Several contemporaries considered Tracy the greatest actor of his era, a sentiment summed up by actor Richard Widmark, who once said, "He's the greatest movie actor there ever was...I've learned more about acting from watching Tracy than in any other way."

Tracy's career earned him an unbelievable number of accolades, and a place in the American Film Institute's Top 10 actors of the 20th century, but it's also an open question how much more he could have accomplished without a litany of health problems brought on by alcohol. Even as he went years at a time without drinking, the effects gradually wore him down physically, and by his early 60's, he needed full-time care, provided mostly by his most famous co-star and lover, Katharine Hepburn. Ironically, his relationship with Hepburn has actually served to overshadow his own acting career among modern viewers, even as his acting abilities remain universally recognized.

Spencer Tracy and Katharine Hepburn: Hollywood's Most Famous Couple profiles the life, career, and legacy of the man deemed by the American Film Institute as one of Hollywood's 10 greatest actors. Along with pictures of important people, places, and events, you will learn about Spencer Tracy like you never have before.

Katharine Hepburn (1907-2003)

"Acting is the most minor of gifts and not a very high-class way to earn a living. After all, Shirley Temple could do it at the age of four." – Katharine Hepburn

Early in her career, there was no actress more controversial than Katharine Hepburn. Late in her career, there was no actress more beloved than Katharine Hepburn. Famously labeled "box office poison" in 1938, it is clear that Hollywood was not prepared for the young Hepburn. Yet, even after being scorned by the general public, Hepburn still retained a magnetism that would endear her to the public for decades to come, and after a tumultuous first decade as an actress, Hepburn became arguably the biggest box office sensation in the industry. Moreover, in an era when most actresses were unable to secure starring roles after reaching middle age, Hepburn remained a leading lady even after turning 60. Hepburn acted in some capacity from the start of the 1930s through the early-1990s, and it is important to view how the nature of Hepburn's roles changed from her youth to old age.

Aside from being one of the most recognized and acclaimed actresses in history, Hepburn's career is also of great importance because she forced Americans to reevaluate their expectations for female behavior, both in films themselves and off the movie set as well. As society began to pay greater attention to the importance of strong roles for women, Hepburn's career gained an even greater importance, and at a time in which women were expected to be passive, she was a fiercely individual figure who offered a daring alternative to the conventions of femininity that had long existed in American culture. Through exploring Hepburn's upbringing and family background, it is possible to gain insight into exactly how Hepburn was endowed with such an iconoclastic spirit. In addition to examining her background, this study considers the broad scope of her career, considering important factors such as how her image evolved over her career.

Spencer Tracy and Katharine Hepburn: Hollywood's Most Famous Couple profiles the life and career of one of America's most iconic actresses. Along with pictures of important people, places, and events, you will learn about Hepburn like you never have before.

Chapter 1: Hellion

"I never would have gone back to school if there had been any other way of learning to read the subtitles in the movies." – Spencer Tracy

When Spencer Tracy was born, his father John had turned himself into a wealthy self-made man who came from a devoutly Catholic family and whose ancestors had come to America from Ireland during the Great Potato Famine. His father and grandfather had made their money working for the expanding American railroad system in Wisconsin, doing well enough to send John all his siblings to St. Mary's High School. John went on to the University of Notre Dame, and two of his three sisters became nuns.

Meanwhile, Caroline Tracy's background could not have been more different from her future husband's. Her family had been in America since colonial times, they had made their money in milling grain, and they were pillars of the First Presbyterian Church. Caroline was a great (and pampered) beauty, and her father was not about to let her marry any Irish Catholic upstart. At the same time, John Tracy's father was not any happier about his son marrying outside his faith. Together, the two fathers agreed that the young couple must not see each other anymore, and to this end, Tracy, Sr. placed both John and his brother Will under a strict 10 o'clock curfew.

To get around this predicament, John's sister Jenny intervened on behalf of the young lovers. She would later recall, "I would sit up on the stairs or at the upstairs window and wait for those two to come home. I would sneak down and open the door so that they would be able to come in the house, and God knows sometimes it was two or three o'clock in the morning and I would have sat there all night. My nerves were ruined when I was a very young girl." Thankfully, Jenny's nerves were not wasted; on August 29, 1894, John and Carrie were wed in her father's home by a Catholic priest. A few days later, the newlyweds packed their belongings and move to LaSalle, where John had taken a job with a new bank.

Unfortunately, John's problems with alcohol, which Carrie must have thought would eventually go away as he got older, cost him his job and drove the young couple back to Freeport within a year. The young couple subsequently moved in with John's family, and it was there that their first son, Carroll Tracy, was born on June 15, 1896. Not long after Carroll's birth, Carrie and John left the crowded Tracy house and moved in with her parents, since their larger home had a staff on hand to see to the needs of both mother and baby. All the while, the couple still wanted a home of their own and finally found one in early 1899 in Merrill Park, a pleasant neighborhood in Milwaukee.

It was in this house that their next child, also a boy, would be born on April 5, 1900. Before Spencer was born, Carrie had wanted a girl and had not even thought of a name for a boy. When Jenny Tracy asked Carrie what the boy would be named, Carrie replied, "I'm so disappointed that he's a boy. He was supposed to be Daisy after my good friend Daisy Spencer." That gave

Jenny the idea of having the boy named Spencer. Once that was settled, Jenny also helped the parents come up with Spencer's middle name while carrying her 17 day old nephew to the St. Rose Catholic Church for the baptism. They decided to honor their sister Bonnie by giving little Spencer the middle name of Bonaventure, thus naming him after a saint.

The two may have had some reason to rethink their decision when the priest, learning that the child he was baptizing would be named Spencer Bonaventure, asked sincerely if the baby was a boy of girl. But they ran into even more trouble when Carrie learned that her newborn son had been saddled with the name of a saint so obscure that she had never heard of him. Instead, she insisted that the baby's birth certificate read "Spencer Bernard Tracy" and thus, at the age of less than three weeks, little Spencer Tracy had experienced his first brush with the incompatibility between who he was and who others thought he should be.

This discrepancy would only become more pronounced as the boy grew older. For instance, Carroll was a quiet and studious boy, and since he was four years older than Spencer, Carrie and John assumed this was how well-bred little boys behaved. However, Spencer was the polar opposite of his brother, preferring to run and tussle and throw things rather than playing quietly. This led his Aunt Emma to once moan, "He's a throwback." Even mothers of other rambunctious little boys noticed Spencer's hyperactivity, and one woman from the neighborhood later remembered, "He was in dresses when I first saw him. He was bubbling with life. I don't believe he ever sat still. I can't remember him sitting down in a chair or reading a book. His brother Carroll … liked to stay inside and listen to the talk of his elders …but Spence was always outside with the boys."

By that time, the family had moved again, this time to a roomy home in the neighborhood of Bay View, just outside of Milwaukee. John Tracy left this home faithfully every Sunday morning and walked with his two young sons to Catholic mass at Immaculate Conception, but church was one of the few places where little Spencer did not get into trouble. The activity of singing, standing, sitting, kneeling, then standing or kneeling again kept him busy, and the beauty and pageantry of the service kept his mind fixed on the altar. Their mutual faith would prove to be a bond between father and son that would last a lifetime, but it was a different case with Spencer's mother. Rejecting her husband's "papist" beliefs, Carrie Tracy was more interested in her son's education, so she enrolled him in the still-new class called "kindergarten" when he was 5 years old. Perhaps not surprisingly, little Spencer did not find his classes on Trowbridge Street as interesting as the mass at church, and he would later recall:

> "I began to show signs of wanderlust at seven. I wandered completely out of the neighborhood and struck up an acquaintance with two delightful companions, Mousie and Rattie. Their father owned a saloon in a very hard-boiled neighborhood. It was a lot more fun playing with them than in was at school. Being sentimentally Irish, that common-enough episode in a kid's life was to have a

lasting effect on my future. For the first time I saw my mother cry over me. I
resolved in an immature way never to make her cry again. I don't mean to initiate
that I became a model boy. I didn't."

During Spencer's early childhood, his family would move two more times, each time living
even closer to school just so Carrie could keep a better eye on Spencer and try to make sure he
got there and back each day without getting into trouble. Even then, however, Spencer got along
better with rougher boys than those in his comfortable neighborhood. He would often bring
these young ruffians home with him, where his mother would fill them up with cheese
sandwiches. Carrie would later remember these times somewhat fondly, explaining to one
reporter:

> "I can honestly say that back of every one of Spencer's exploits was something
> fine like sympathy, generosity, affection, pride, or ambition. There was not a
> mean bone through in him. True, he broke windows with the same alarming and
> expensive regularity boys do today. And he would get embroiled in fights to help
> a friend, fights, incidentally, from which Carroll invariably would have to rescue
> him because he was so thin and sickly a child until he was 14 that he could never
> finish on his own what he was quick to start or join in…even though it meant
> added work for me and bigger bills for John to pay at the stores, neither of us could
> find it in our hearts to punish or discourage him from such a fine philosophy."

Unfortunately, the rest of Carrie's side of the family was not so tolerant. Spencer and Carroll
spent summers back in Freemont with both sets of their grandparents, and while Spencer's
parents were more tolerant of the boy's shenanigans, his grandparents tended to try to find
activities for Spencer that got him out of the house and out from under their feet. This often
meant giving the boy a nickel and sending him to see a silent picture show. It was here, in the
darkened theaters, that Spencer first discovered the joy of being lost in a story.

When Spencer was about 9 years old, his parents became sufficiently concerned about his
behavior to make a major change in his education. They removed him from the local public
school and enrolled him in St. John's Cathedral School, trusting the Dominican Sisters who ran
the school to mold and shape their wayward son into a more disciplined young man.
Surprisingly, Spencer actually thrived at the rigorous Catholic school. For one thing, serving as
an altar boy gave him his first outlet for public performance; while he was sincerely devout, he
also enjoyed the experience of putting on the "costume" of robe and surplice, carrying the props
of incense and candles, and reciting the lines of the mass in response to the intoning priest.
During this period, life at home also improved, in no small part due to the fact that John finally
came to terms with his alcoholism and completely gave up drinking. Unable to socialize at the
local bar anymore, he stayed home in the evenings and the family had friends over instead. In
the days before radio or television, talented children were often called upon to perform for adults

before going upstairs to bed, and Spencer thrived during this time by learning magic tricks and small vaudeville style acts to perform for company. He also put on shows in the family's basement, charging his friends one or two pins to attend a performance.

Spencer continued to perform when given a chance, but he also turned his mind to earning money. He got his first job as a lamplighter in 1912, and he continued to work at random odd jobs even when his family moved to a wealthy neighborhood in Milwaukee in 1916. Now that he seemed more settled and responsible, his parents felt secure enough about his future to remove him from the sisters' charge and enroll him in Wauwatosa High, a local public school. However, this proved to be a disaster, and Spencer soon flunked out. He later explained his failure, "I might have enjoyed school if I had been doing the thing I wanted to do. My trouble was not having a definite ambition or goal on which to concentrate. I wanted to be doing something that would hold my interest, but I had no idea what it would be."

Needless to say, Spencer was soon sent back to Catholic school, first St. John's, and when the family moved to Kansas City, Spencer was sent to Rockhurst Academy, a Jesuit school that soon straightened him out. He explained, "I remember Rockhurst as a big building and I remember pursuing to the best of my abilities the study of Latin and geometry. I also remember that there were some boys at Rockhurst and in Kansas City who were mighty good fighters." Unfortunately, John Tracy's job played out in 1917, so the family returned to Milwaukee and Spencer was enrolled in the exclusive Jesuit school Marquette Academy. Now mature enough to balance his studies and other pursuits, Spencer did well in school, and he also established an amateur drama company with fellow future actor Bill O'Brien. Meanwhile, he also remembered feeling like he may have found his first true brush with a potential vocation, later saying, "The influence is strong, very strong, intoxicating. The priest are all such superior men---heroes. You want to be like them---we all did. Every guy in the school probably thought some more or less about trying for the cloth. You lie in dark and see yourself as Monsignor Tracy, Cardinal Tracy, Bishop Tracy, Archbishop---I'm getting goose flesh!

Once the United States entered World War I, however, Spencer began looking forward to new and more distant horizons. He explained, "Well, it was wartime. 1917. And the uniform seemed more appropriate than the habit. Or more glamorous. Everybody was joining up. So we did, too. Caroll and Pat and I went into the Navy. And I guess that's where Cardinal Tracy started turning into Admiral Tracy." The Pat he was referring to was his good friend and fellow actor Pat O'Brien, who was at Marquette Academy with Tracy.

Pat O'Brien with Anne Jeffreys in *Riffraff* (1947)

Eventually, Spencer, who was admittedly "itching for a chance to go and see some excitement", decided to lie about his age and enlist. Tracy recalled that he "knew very well where there was a U.S. Marines recruiting station, for I'd seen it lots of times before", so one day he walked into the office and told the man at the desk, "I want to join the Marines." However, he found himself unable to lie about his age when the time came, so he ultimately waited for the four months it would take him to turn 18. By the time this happened, recruitment of soldiers was at a fevered pitch, and Pat O'Brien later remembered, "The bands played, the drill parades started, the Liberty Bond drives were on, and Spence and myself and some of the others left school one afternoon and went downtown to the enlistment headquarters of the Navy." While O'Brien ended up rethinking his enlistment, Spencer signed up, and though the war ended before he saw any fighting, Tracy would always praise the effect basic training had on his life: "The training, the discipline, and the healthy life not only did me good physically but mentally as well. I realized for the first time that a man must make his own way in life, that he must assume certain responsibilities, and that a man can't receive too much education, because the Navy demand alert minds."

Tracy in 1919

Tracy was discharged from the Navy on February 19, 1919, with a rank of seaman first class, after which he joined the rest of the released veterans in looking for work. Thanks to his father's connections, he soon secured a job as a truck driver, but his father had bigger dreams for him and wanted him to attend college. This required Tracy to give up the freedom of the open road and return to high school. He enrolled in Northwestern Military and Naval College and stayed there just long enough to gather the credits needed to graduate and get into college. Thanks to his father's hard work to track down every possible academic credit Spencer might have, and to ferret out "war credits" granted to high school students who had left school to enter the military, Spencer Tracy finally graduated from high school and entered Ripon College in February 1921. He was about to turn 21, and he later recounted how he had reached this point in life, "Back there in Milwaukee, I don't remember ever seeing an actor and I certainly never thought about it when I was in the Navy. In fact, when I was in the Navy I thought I wanted to be a sailor. And maybe if the family hadn't been so dead set on me finishing high school, I would've stayed in the Navy, but when I got out, I did go back to high school and then---I don't know---automatically, I suppose, college."

At first, Tracy planned to focus his attention on the sciences with an eye to entering medical school, but his public speaking classes changed all that. He excelled in this area, leading one of his professors to later say, "I remember very vividly the occasions when we were working on problems of impression and his speeches would actually leave the class in tears. His dramatic instinct was shown in his surpassing ability in telling a story. There was always the proper sequence of events, the gradual rise to a climax, the carefully-chosen ending." Public speaking led naturally to acting, and Tracy landed the lead in the college's production of *The Truth*. Clark Graham, who directed the piece, remembered Tracy having "a clipped firmness of expression indicating poise, self-control, and confidence." The play was a huge success thanks to Tracy, whose stage presence in one tense scene was so powerful that it frightened even his leading lady. According to a review in the college newspaper, "Mr. Tracy proved himself a consistent and unusually strong actor in his most difficult straight part. His steadiness, his reserve strength and suppressed emotion were a pleasant surprise to all who heard him as [Tom] Warder." As the curtain rang down that opening night, John Tracy's hopes for his son graduating college died and Spencer Tracy's plan to act was born.

When he was passed over for the lead in the school's next play, Spencer teamed up with a friend to form their own theatrical troupe. They staged *The Valiant*, with Tracy playing a convicted murderer determined to protect his kid sister from knowing who he really was. He shocked the audience by reciting the details of a battle in which the brother supposedly died heroically, only to then turn on a dime and recall the poetry the two had shared as children. The reviews were gushing, with one journalist commenting that Tracy played his role "in such a masterful way that the audience felt with him the emotions he portrayed."

After that, the crew, now informally calling themselves "The Campus Players", took their show on the road and performed *The Valiant* for local campus audiences. Tracy later told a reporter what happened next:

> "I must have been a real pain in the ass arguing all the time with everybody because one of the professors there finally stopped me and sucked me into being on the debating team. From there I suppose it was only a short hop to the drama club. Then, well, you know how it is. Every guy starts to tell you how good you are and you start to believe it. Even so, nothing would've happened probably if our debating

team hadn't been invited to debate up at Bowdoin College in Maine, and on the way we had to stop off in New York for a day. And I went over to the American Academy of Dramatic Art---I'd seen about it somewhere---and auditioned for Franklin Sargent. They must've been pretty short of men because he offered me a scholarship. When I got out of college, I went to New York and took him up on it. Pat was there, too. Pat O'Brien. We'd known each other as kids. We had a room together somewhere in the West Fifties. We were in the same class. Neither one of us very impressive. I don't know why. We sure tried."

Tracy began classes with the American Academy of Dramatic Art in April 1922, and much to his own surprise and pleasure, he was allowed to join the senior class there and thus participate in the local stock company. His first play, *The Wedding Guest*, was well-received when it opened in October 1922, and just three months later, Tracy found himself on Broadway for the first time, playing a silent robot in the show *R.U.R.* A few months later, in March 1923, he graduated from AADA and launched his career as a "real actor." He would later praise the academy for shaping his career, saying, "I shall always be grateful to the American Academy of Dramatic Arts for what I was taught there---the value of sincerity and simplicity, unembellished and un-intellectualized."

Chapter 2: A Childhood of Gaiety and Tragedy

Katharine Houghton Hepburn was born May 12, 1907 in Hartford, Connecticut, the second child of the family and the younger sister of her brother Tom, who was two years older. Both Katharine and Tom were named after their parents: Katharine (Kit) Martha Houghton and Thomas Norval Hepburn. They had been married three years earlier and lived in an upscale house in Hartford.

The fact that Kit and Thomas named their children after themselves reflects the strong pride that they held in themselves, as well as their hopes that their children would one day follow in their footsteps. Much has been made of the zaniness of the Hepburn family, but Kit and Thomas were relatively conservative in the premium they placed on their family heritage. After all, the Hepburns were among the more affluent families in their Hartford neighborhood. Though Kit did not work, she came from a family background replete with immense wealth, and while Thomas's pedigree was more humble, his profession as a surgeon at Hartford Hospital paid handsomely. Katharine was thus born into a comfortable background and a setting of great privilege.

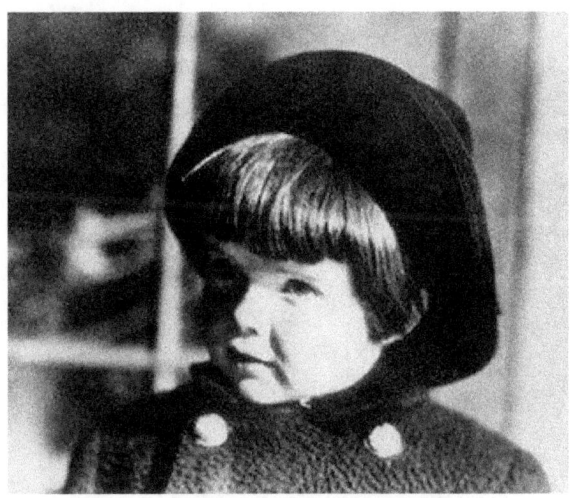

Katharine as a young girl

In addition to the affluent background, Katharine grew up in a very tight-knit household, and her parents would have a tremendous impact on her life, both acting as a strong support system and influencing her with their own beliefs. Kit was born in 1878, and her family owned the Corning Incorporated glass works. Their possession of this company made them extraordinarily wealthy, and they lived a luxurious existence in Buffalo, New York. The family fortune amassed from Corning Incorporated glass works effectively ensured Kit would not be relegated to working, nor have to worry about money, for the duration of her life. But despite her blessed childhood, her life turned somber in 1892, when her father committed suicide. Then Kit's mother was diagnosed with rapidly-developing stomach cancer shortly after her husband's death, and she passed away in 1894. At this point, Kit and her siblings were placed under the supervision of their uncle, a transition that necessitated a move from Buffalo to Boston. Even though Kit was already 16 years old at the time of her mother's death, the move to Boston would have a formative effect on her, imparting her with a New England sensibility that she would retain as an adult and would later impress upon her children.

Kit

Kit was also very progressive, a trait she had obtained from her mother, who impressed upon her the importance of receiving a college education. Kit and her two sisters all attended Bryn Mawr College, and after graduating, Kit traveled to Europe for a year, where she quickly became fluent in French. It is believed that she later received a graduate degree in chemistry or physics, although it has also been asserted that her advanced degree was in art history. Regardless of the exact discipline, Kit's pre-marital life reflects the emphasis on education and worldly endeavor that she would later impress upon her children.

Meanwhile, Thomas Norval Hepburn did not come from as privileged a background as his young wife, but his family did have indirect ties to Mary, Queen of Scots, and they lived a very comfortable existence. A large, burly, redheaded Scotsman, he attended Randolph-Macon College, and subsequently Johns Hopkins University for medical school. At a time in which few doctors acted as specialized surgeons, Thomas practiced exclusively as a urologist. Like his wife, he also appreciated traveling, and he stayed in Germany for a short while after meeting his future wife to serve in a surgical unit in Germany. After settling down in Hartford, Hepburn would remain there for the rest of his career, raising all six of his children in Hartford and their summer home in Old Saybrook, Connecticut.

For all of their wealth and Thomas's skill as a doctor, the most noteworthy aspect of the

Hepburns was their political progressiveness. While the majority of wealthy individuals during that period were staunch conservatives, the Hepburns were effusive in their liberal beliefs and championed the rights of underrepresented groups, particularly women. Kit was the head of the Connecticut Women Suffrage Association, and when Katharine was young, Kit would take her daughter to women's suffrage demonstrations. Kit had connections with many of the most prominent activists and intellectuals along the East Coast, and it was not uncommon for her to invite intellectual luminaries for tea or dinner in order to discuss suffrage or various events of the time period. This influence on Katharine was apparent as late as her 1981 interview with Barbara Walters, in which she said, "I have not lived as a woman. I have lived as a man…I've just done what I damn well wanted to and I made enough money to support myself."

While Thomas was not the public activist that his wife was, he was similarly progressive in his political views. As a urologist, he was a firm proponent in the use of contraceptives; both he and his wife were atheists who advocated the use of birth control for women. When they would have guests over to their house who did not share their liberal views, they were frank in dismissing their views and could often be condescending. Thus, they had qualities that made them both easy to appreciate (their firm belief in civil rights for all) but also difficult and polarizing, a balance that Katharine would clearly inherit herself. Katharine also embraced these views, at one point saying, "I'm an atheist, and that's it. I believe there's nothing we can know except that we should be kind to each other and do what we can for other people."

Kit and Thomas were certainly intimidating figures, but they raised their daughter in a nurturing, accepting environment, and Katharine would remain deeply attached to them for the rest of their lives. Later in life she would note: "No one does it alone. Your success belongs to the people who are holding you up. I can only say that I am the product of adorable people. I've been so lucky, just so lucky." Katharine also credited her grandmother for her mother's ways, stating, "My beautiful Grandmother -- Caroline Garlinghouse - I never met her but I have followed many of her ideas - through my mother."

The tight-knit nature of the family stemmed not only from the loving affection Katharine's parents exhibited toward their daughter but also the insular environment in which she was raised. While her parents led an active social life and there were frequent visitors to the Hepburn household, Katharine was mostly isolated from the greater neighborhood as a young child. Instead of matriculating in a pre-school and kindergarten, she remained at home, where she was schooled under the supervision of Kit, and even after reaching an age when most children would enroll in elementary school, Katharine and her brother were tutored at home. This unquestionably contributed to her self-acknowledged selfishnesses; Katharine later admitted that she was "a me me me person" early in life, and she confessed it was also the reason she did not want to have kids: "I would have been a terrible mother because I'm basically a very selfish human being."

It was not until 1917, when she was already 10 years old, that she would enroll in a proper elementary school: the Oxford School in Hartford. The tiny school had just 90 students, but it provided Katharine with her first daily interaction with other neighborhood children. She began to develop friendships with others, but the fact that she had lived such a sheltered existence early in life imbued her with an independent spirit and sense of familial elitism that would brand her later in life.

The fact Hepburn did not attend an elementary school until she was 10 might lead many to believe that she led a lonely existence until that age, but that was hardly the case. She and her older brother Tom were best friends and acted almost like twins. At a young age, her brother fell ill with a particularly dangerous form of fever that would leave him susceptible to bouts of depression, yet he generally exhibited the same infectious enthusiasm held by his sister. When noting that Katharine and Tom were especially close, it is important to distinguish that Tom was not effeminate in his manner but rather that Katharine was very much the tomboy, another quality that would define her as a young actress. In fact, as a young child she insisted on being referred to as "Jimmy" and wore her hair short, to the extent that people looking at pictures of her childhood would have difficulty ascertaining her gender. Mr. Hepburn stressed the importance of physical exercise, and the children were encouraged to be strong, physically capable adults, a quality that was hindered when Katharine's brother fell ill with fever but was generally the case with all of the Hepburn children. Mr. Hepburn also had his children take frigidly cold baths, believing that the cold temperature stimulated the mind.

In addition to Tom, Katharine was kept company by the brothers and sisters that followed her: Richard, Robert, Marion, and Margaret. The younger siblings were born over the first 13 years of Katharine's life, and she would take on an almost motherly role with her younger siblings, a dynamic that is perhaps ironic in light of the fact that she would later eschew having children as an adult. However, despite the affection she felt for her younger siblings, Katharine remained far closer to her older brother than to her younger brothers and sisters. This dynamic is understandable considering that there was a four year age gap separating Katharine from the next-oldest child, her brother Richard (Dick). Always a precocious child, Hepburn was more interested in spending time with her older sibling than with caring for the younger ones. In academic matters, Tom set an example with his strong intellect, and in athletic endeavors he was her sparring partner. All of the members of the Hepburn family were exceptionally close, but the bond between Katharine and Tom was truly inseparable and one of a kind.

The Hepburn Family, with Katharine at the lower left

One of the most welcome developments that took place during Hepburn's childhood was the purchase of the family's summer home in 1913. Located in Fenwick, a division of Old Saybrook, Connecticut, the house has been mythologized as the locus for the Hepburn family headquarters, and it is definitely fair to associate it with Katharine's identity. Referring to Fenwick later in life, Hepburn would note, "Fenwick is and always has been my other paradise. It is at the mouth of the Connecticut River about forty-five miles from Hartford. Dad discovered it in 1913." Her statement suggests both her tremendous affection toward the family's residence and the reverence she held for her father, referring to him in terms that likened him to an explorer. In any event, Fenwick was the site of great happiness for Katharine, offering an idyllic summer lifestyle that was complete with numerous opportunities for enjoyment. She could play golf and tennis on a daily basis, and she eventually excelled at both.

The summer Home at Fenwick

At Fenwick, Hepburn also developed an interest in show business, with a fascination for both film and theater. As a child, she would attend roughly one film per week, and she was captivated by silent cinema. During the first half of the 20th century, movie theaters seemed like grand palaces, and Hepburn was in awe of the enormity of the image on such big screens, as well as the fantastical narratives and even the ornate intertitles. In addition to her burgeoning love for film, Hepburn was enthralled with the theater; in the family dining room at Fenwick, she and neighborhood children would stage theatrical productions. Life at Fenwick was a summer paradise, replete with a lifestyle of leisure from which Hepburn could never fully distance herself even as an adult.

It is fortunate that Hepburn embraced her family's lifestyle, since it certainly ran counter to social convention and was eclectic. In fact, the family lifestyle is at the heart of a "Hepburn myth" that developed early in Katharine's film career. The Hepburns delighted in living a lifestyle that was antithetical to the standard routines practiced by other families. Mr. and Mrs. Hepburn treated their children as equals, and from an early age Katharine was fond of asserting her individuality. To this end, Anne Edward explains:

> "The Hepburn lifestyle at Fenwick and at their West Hartford home was organized chaos. 'The Doctor says he runs the family, Mrs. Hepburn thinks she does, and Kate *knows* she does,' an observer once said. All the Hepburns functioned on sheer nervous energy. There were no schedules. Breakfast could well be served at noon, lunch at four, and dinner at nine. Visitors always seemed to arrive in the middle of a meal, and there was a great deal of walking about the dining room, plate in hand, as one Hepburn found the distance to another inhibiting to a lively conversation that could have had as a topic anything from the atomic bomb to birth control. The only

note of formality about dinner was the carving of the roast, done by Mr. Hepburn with surgical control."

As this description makes plain, the only structure in the Hepburn household was a persistent lack of structure. The unpredictability of the subject of conversation also demonstrated the absence of any filter relating to social decorum. Through engaging dinner guests in serious discussions of sensitive topics, from politics to the need for contraception, the family established a bold identity and a spirit of social defiance. One (possibly apocryphal) anecdote asserts that the Hepburn parents were fond of parading around the household nude, encouraged their children to do so as well, and were unabashed in their public displays of affection. Such familial intimacy might have endeared Katharine to her parents, but it also made it that much more difficult to integrate into more standardized environments of social decorum later in life. Regardless of the developments that would take place in Katharine's life there, Fenwick remained her hallowed ground.

Hepburn's upbringing was idyllic growing up, but in 1921, when she was 13 years old, an event occurred that would both radically alter the family and send her into a deep depression for several years. Katharine and her older brother had a ritual in which they would visit their mother's longtime friend (from her time at Bryn Mawr) in New York City for weekends. However, during one of these excursions, Tom hung himself in the middle of the night, and Katharine found Tom dead after waking up the next morning. The event was traumatic enough in its own right, but it was only exacerbated when the local newspaper reported that the death was possibly caused by murder, with Katharine as the primary suspect. The insinuation of murder was almost immediately dropped, yet it has been argued that this event inaugurated the tumultuous relationship with the press that Hepburn would retain throughout her life.

The reasons for why Tom would take his own life at such a young age remain unclear. Tom never left a suicide note, and it is possible that he did not intend to kill himself. His father was fond of relaying a story concerning a former classmate of his who had been able to contort his throat muscles so as to avoid dying while having a rope tied around his neck, and Katharine's brother may have been attempting to emulate this technique. However, it is also important to remember that Tom had long suffered from bouts of depression as a result of the fever that had placed him in critical condition as a young child. As a result, it is possible that he was simply overcome by a temporary episode of depression.

Regardless of the reason, Tom's death had a profound effect on Katharine, since she had no idea that he was even depressed, let alone suicidal. Devastated by his death, she terminated her enrollment in the Oxford School and was once again tutored at the family home. She and her brother had previously been inseparable, and after his death she became more isolated than ever before, as evidenced by her later statement: "Onliness is my word for what I called my philosophy for life…It's a word I made up for myself when my teenage brother hanged himself."

It has also been argued that the death of her brother would eventually make her even more driven to succeed in life, as she realized the importance of living for herself and maximizing her potential in life. Tom's death thus had the effect of not only sending her into her own depression but of making her become more individualistic. It was no doubt painful at first, but she would grow to embrace it as an adult.

By the time Hepburn turned 17, she had at least partially overcome the depression that had subsumed her in the wake of her brother's premature death. Physically, she was fully developed and no longer the tomboy she had been during her youth, but this did not mean that her body was of standard proportion. Hepburn is not only remembered for her unusual personality but also her striking physicality. She was 5'8 and relatively flat-chested, with a body that lacked the curvature that defined female beauty at the time. She also did not possess the waifish figure that would emerge over the following decades, and yet there was no denying that she was still strikingly attractive. Anne Edwards offers a comprehensive description of the fully-developed Hepburn: "Her wispy, brick-red hair framed a haughty, sharp-boned face. Tall and lanky, with a loping gait and broomstick posture, she also possessed an overgenerous mouth, widely-spaced, piercing gray-blue eyes, flaring nostrils, high cheekbones, and a strange voice—nasal, part-Bostonian (learned from her mother), part affectation, part Virginia belle (learned from her father)."

Hepburn's body was unconventional, and given Edwards's description, it would perhaps be most accurate to say that Hepburn's beauty was actually derived from its masculine characteristics. After all, her broad shoulders, tall legs, and high cheekbones defined her more than her breasts or curves. Hepburn was a startling figure, and even after entering Hollywood, which was notorious for "improving" the appearance of its actors and actresses, Hepburn's appearance retained a gender-bending quality that made her particularly arresting and challenging to audiences.

Hepburn's college yearbook photo at Bryn Mawr

Hepburn's unique appearance also happened to correlate with her fierce sense of individuality. Hepburn had largely eschewed social contact with others her age since ending her studies at the Oxford School following her brother's death four years earlier. From time to time, she had engaged in minor romantic relationships, but she had never maintained a steady boyfriend, and her education did not involve any interpersonal interaction. This dynamic inevitably changed almost out of necessity. Katharine may have been resolute in her love for her family and home, but her parents also made clear that she had to receive an advanced education, and they were determined that she enrolled in college. In the 1920s, it was most common for women to attend all-girls schools, and 17 year old Katharine followed in her mother's footsteps by enrolling at Bryn Mawr College in 1924.

Hepburn's tenure at Bryn Mawr is well-documented as an example of her elitism, but much of her time there consisted of defiantly acting in opposition to the accepted norms for student behavior. During the fall semester following her matriculation, she famously wore an elaborate dress into the dining hall, an act that resulted in a classmate's proclamation that she was a "self-conscious beauty." Embarrassed by the event but too proud and shy to reform to the conventions of student life at Bryn Mawr, Hepburn developed a reclusive lifestyle. Using a generous stipend that her father sent her each month, Hepburn ate most of her meals at restaurants, or simply made cereal inside her dormitory room. At one point, she was even suspended for smoking in her room.

Her efforts to evade the attention of her classmates were in vain, however, partly because she made herself stand out even while attempting to keep her distance. Following a routine she had developed during her upbringing, Hepburn slept at odd hours, waking up and showering at 4:00 in the morning, and in class, she eschewed contemporary fashions and instead wore oddly-colored, elaborate outfits that drew attention. Despite her shyness and apparent dislike for attention, one is left to wonder why she chose to dress in such a way if she was ungrateful for the attention that resulted. It seems more likely that she must have enjoyed at least some aspect of drawing attention, or she would have simply conformed to the routines of her peers. Either way, this social dynamic at Bryn Mawr foreshadowed the uneasy relationship she would cultivate with the public later in life, pushing against attention while acting in a manner that inevitably ensured she would be noticed.

For all of her difficulties adjusting to college life, Hepburn did eventually make friends and find her niche. One summer during her time at Bryn Mawr (the exact year remains ambiguous, although it is likely that it was following her Junior year), she and a circle of friends traveled to London and Paris. Academically, her grades were quite poor during her first year, but over time she improved her grades dramatically, and after realizing that she wanted to become an actress, Katharine became aware that in order to act in any plays, she needed to maintain a strong grade point average. This motivation served as the impetus for her commitment to her academics, and she would eventually major in both history and philosophy.

More importantly, Katharine starred in a series of plays at Bryn Mawr, most notably the leading role in a production of *The Woman in the Moon* (1928), for which she received positive reviews. By the time of her graduation, Hepburn had little doubt that she wanted to become an actress. The decision to act seems intuitive in hindsight, but it was met with great scorn by Hepburn's father. Tom had long hoped that his daughter would become a doctor, although this was hardly realistic considering her background in history and philosophy. Considering her father's disapproval, Hepburn's initial inspiration for acting is unclear, and it is possible that the career choice was made simply out of an attempt to provoke her father. It is also important to remember that Hepburn was really under no pressure to find gainful employment, because her family remained immensely wealthy, and she knew that if her career fell through she could always return to Fenwick and her family.

Chapter 3: The Stage

"There were times when my pants were so thin, I could sit on a dime and know if it was heads or tails." – Spencer Tracy

"If you obey all the rules, you will miss all the fun." – Katharine Hepburn

Unfortunately for both Tracy and Hepburn, the real world of acting was not as easy to break into as college shows had been. After graduating, he moved to White Plains, New York and joined a local acting company there called the Wood Players, but much to his surprise and consternation, he was not immediately given leads in every play. Instead, he was given small roles that the director felt were more suitable to his experience (or lack thereof). Quickly becoming disappointed with the direction his career was taking, Tracy sought comfort in the arms of Louise Treadwell, a fellow actress and member of the Wood Players. The two would continue dating off and on until they were married on September 10, 1923.

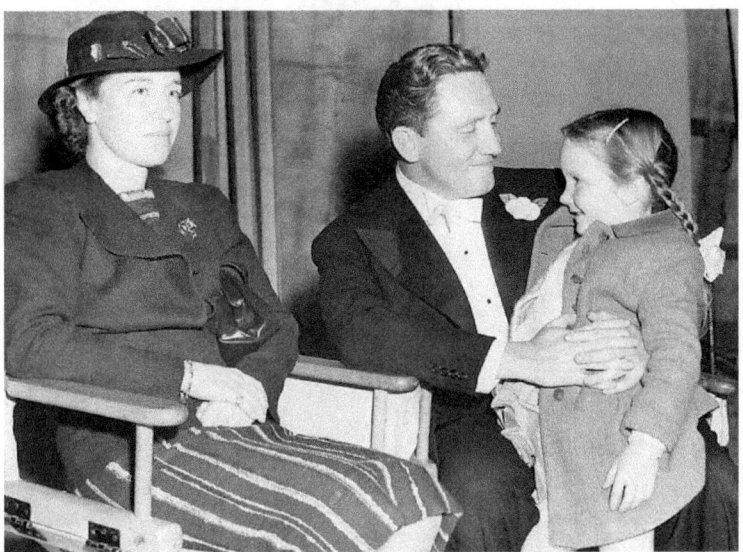

Louise and Spencer Tracy

During this time, Tracy moved to Cincinnati, but he quickly found he had the same problem there that had plagued him in New York: there were plenty of aspiring actors and few good parts. Right after he and Louise married, he landed a small role on Broadway in *A Royal Fandango*, appearing with Ethel Barrymore, the first star he had ever worked with, but the play closed after only 25 performances. Although this was probably due more to the stars' failures than Tracy's, he later admitted that his ego "took an awful beating", and he almost quit acting altogether.

It was perhaps during this trying time that Tracy cheated on his wife for the first time, but regardless of when it first occurred, infidelity would continue to plague their marriage for as long as he lived. Now a married man with a baby on the way, Tracy moved his young family to Winnipeg in January 1924, where he landed his first professional leading role. When that gig ended almost as soon as it began, Tracy returned to America and went to work for William H Wright, a well-known stock manager who was putting together a new production starring a well-known actress named Selena Royle. Tracy and Royle had good chemistry, and after the play proved a success, Tracy's performance also caught the attention of another Broadway producer who offered him the lead in *The Sheepman*. Ultimately, the play opened poorly in Connecticut and closed without ever reaching Broadway.

Selena Royle

When Spencer's son John, was born in June 1924, he considered settling down and trying to be a good father, but Louise knew the pressure her husband was under and therefore was reluctant to share with him the news that John was deaf. She first hid her suspicions, and then the doctor's confirmation, until after the baby's first birthday, but when Tracy noticed that his son was not learning to talk like other children his age, Louise had to share her secret with her husband. Spencer was inconsolable, believing that his son's deafness was somehow a punishment for his own adultery, but instead of trying to make up for his perceived wrong by showering the boy with extra attention, Tracy withdrew from his family and spent more time away from home. Things did not improve even when their second child, a girl they named after Louise's mother, was born in July 1932. It is indicative of his mixed feelings about the children that Tracy, a devoted if not devout Catholic, allowed them to be raised Episcopalians by their mother instead of in his own faith.

Returning to what he knew, Tracy made a few more plays with local stock companies until 1926, when George M. Cohan offered Tracy a role in a play called *Yellow*. By this time, Tracy had made up his mind that if he failed one more time as an actor, he would leave the stage altogether and get a "real job." Fortunately for both Tracy and the world, *Yellow* was a rousing success; upon opening on September 21, it was well-received and ran for over 130 performances. This was the beginning of a long and profitable friendship between Tracy and Cohan, and Tracy would later claim, "I'd have quit the stage completely if it hadn't been for George M. Cohan." For his own part, Cohan called Tracy "the best goddamned actor I've ever seen!"

Cohan

Cohan was so pleased with Tracy's performance in *Yellow* that he had another part written especially for Tracy in his next play, *The Baby Cyclone*. When that play opened on Broadway in September 1927, it became Tracy's first big hit. Next came *Whispering Friends*, and in 1928, Tracy took on a role in *Conflict* after the other star, Clark Gable, had to drop out.

That same year, Hepburn was determined to succeed in the industry, and the day after graduating, she headed to Baltimore in search of an acting job. After arriving there, Hepburn's first stop involved meeting with Edwin H. Knopf, who ran a stock theater company. Realizing that Katharine had no formal training in acting, Knopf was leery of hiring her, but he ultimately acquiesced, and immediately after joining Knopf's company, Hepburn acted in a string of modest productions. The first of these was *The Czarina* (1928), and successful reviews in that led to a role in *Printed Word* (1928), as well as a subsequent production. In these roles, it became clear that Hepburn possessed a strong magnetism that could captivate an audience, but her lack of training was exposed by her harsh, high-pitched voice. In order to remedy her vocal deficiencies, she worked with a vocal instructor in Baltimore, and after receiving instruction, she returned to New York and appeared in a string of plays.

Although Hepburn's arresting appearance helped secure roles for her, she still lacked professionalism, frequently arriving late for performances and forgetting her lines. Her most prominent debacle came during production of *The Big Pond*. Hepburn had been an understudy to an actress who suddenly became unavailable, thrusting her into the leading role in the major theatrical production. In the show's first production, she forgot her lines and was fired. Hepburn wanted to become an actress, but it would be several years before she approached acting with the requisite professionalism needed to succeed. Her lack of professionalism is ironic in light of the fact that people who encountered her later in her career considered her one of the hardest workers in Hollywood, director Stanley Kramer said of her, "Work, work, work. She can work till everyone drops."

Hepburn's personal life also changed in December of 1928, when she married Ludlow Ogden Smith. She had become acquainted with Smith while at Bryn Mawr and was good friends with him, but the marriage was still a major surprise. Smith was 8 years older than Hepburn, and the two also had significantly different personalities. Smith was a socialite, and Katharine was anything but that. From the start, their marriage was deeply unsuccessful. Charles Hingham explained, "The marriage was a disaster. Kate had such a horror for domesticity that the whole experience was a nightmare. She managed to persuade Luddy to call himself Ogden Ludlow, since she hated the idea of being called Kate Smith. She also had him shift his base from Philadelphia to New York and moved with him into a tiny apartment on East Thirty-Ninth Street. They were drastically unhappy there."

The marriage was clearly a bad fit, but it was also evidence that Hepburn was uncomfortable with social norms like marriage, and the manner in which she managed to subvert established conventions. Making her husband change his name and relocate reflect a degree of female agency that was simply not exhibited often in the '20s. At the same time, it is fair to conclude that Hepburn's refusal to make compromises for her husband likely contributed to the disintegration of their relationship. With her career just beginning to flourish, Hepburn was unable to abdicate her career, even if it was unreasonable to expect her husband to give up his profession she continued to make a paltry sum as an actress. After just three weeks together, they separated, even though they would not actually get a divorce until 1934. Despite the brevity of the marriage, the split was amicable, and Luddy continued to subsidize Hepburn even after separating. Years down the road, Hepburn would express deep gratitude toward him for his financial and moral assistance throughout her early career.

Although the marriage has always been overshadowed by her later relationship with Spencer Tracy, Hepburn's marriage to Luddy remains of interest for the way in which it foreshadowed the persona and reputation Katharine would subsequently acquire in Hollywood. Despite submitting to the most patriarchal of institutions in marriage, it was Hepburn who held greater authority in the marriage, a dynamic that was inconceivable in real life in 1928 but not inconceivable in one of her later films.

After separating from Luddy, Katharine's theater career began to reach greater prominence. From 1929-1932, she appeared in *Death Takes a Holiday* (1929), *A Month in the Country* (1929), *Art and Mrs. Bottle* (1931), and *The Animal Kingdom* (1931). At the same time, she continued to face adversity. She only appeared in *Art and Mrs. Bottle* after being fired and rehired when the playwright couldn't find another actress; the playwright described Hepburn in less than glowing terms: "She looks a fright, her manner is objectionable, and she has no talent." Hepburn had hoped *The Animal Kingdom* would be her vehicle to stardom, so her hopes were undoubtedly dashed when she was let go after that production, but she caught her first major break when she appeared in the lead role in a Broadway production of *The Warrior's Husband* (1932). The role featured Hepburn as a female warrior and allowed her to make full use of the athletic physique she had honed since childhood thanks to her father's insistence. The show ran between March and June of 1932, and Hepburn received great acclaim for her performance; New York World-Telegram critic Richard Garland wrote of her, "It's been many a night since so glowing a performance has brightened the Broadway scene."

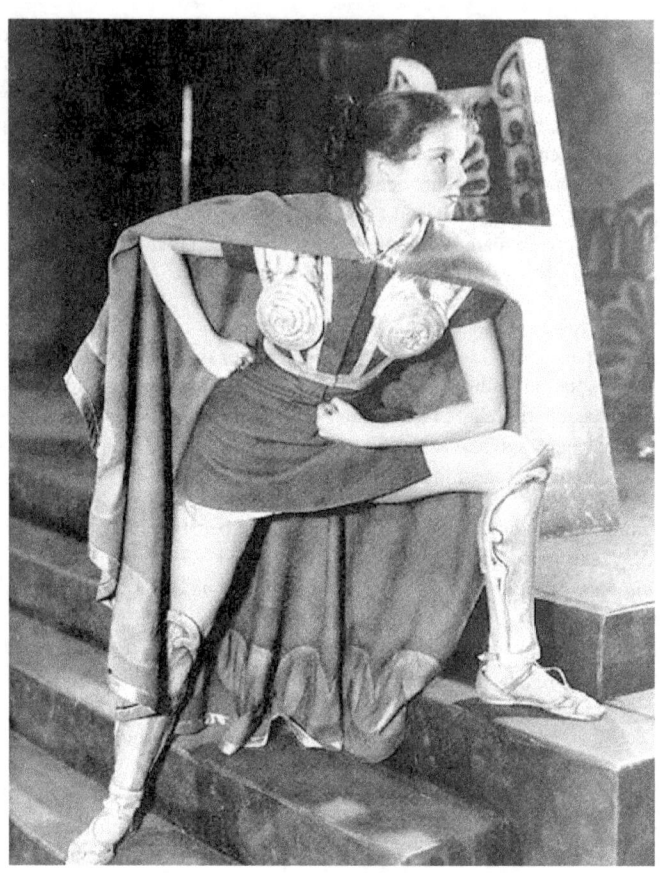

Hepburn in *The Warrior's Husband*

Most importantly, the play caught the attention of Hollywood agent Leland Hayward, who subsequently encouraged Hepburn to audition for the Hollywood film *A Bill of Divorcement* (1932). It's also believed that Hayward subsequently proposed to Hepburn, but that she refused to marry him because it would impede her career. After winning the part, she was signed to a contract of $1500 per week, a salary considered exorbitant for an inexperienced actress during the early 1930s. Hepburn had submitted the figure only half-expecting that RKO, the studio producing the film, would accept. However, director George Cukor, who would later direct a number of Hepburn's most famous films, was impressed with her test footage and pushed the studio's hand in casting her. He later explained his reaction to seeing her test footage by describing her as an "odd creature…unlike anybody I'd ever heard." The contract lasted for a minimum of three weeks, so in July 1932, Hepburn ventured west to California for the first time.

Leland Hayward

George Cukor

Meanwhile, Tracy continued to give solid performances on stage, which led to him landing the lead in *Dread*, written by Owen Davis, the famous Pulitzer Prize winning dramatist. *Dread* might very well have been Tracy's big break had it not opened on October 28, 1929, the day before Wall Street collapsed and the Great Depression began.

Concerned about his ability to find work in such a bad economy, Tracy considered returning home to Milwaukee and his family, but before he could he was contacted in early 1930 about a lead in a play called *The Last Mile*. This time, he would play a serial killer waiting on death row for execution. The producer who hired him, Herman Shimla, later said that he chose Tracy because "beneath the surface, there was a man of passion, violence, sensitivity and desperation: no ordinary man, and just the man for the part." His choice was a good one, and when *The Last Mile* opened in February, Tracy was given a standing ovation that lasted for 14 curtain calls. The play went on to run for more than 280 performances.

Around this time, directors were coming from Hollywood to scout actors for motion pictures. It was the beginning of a new era, with sound pictures replacing silent films, and Tracy got small parts in two shorts called *Taxi Talks* and *The Hard Guy*, but he initially had little interest in making movies. Though he "had no ambition in that direction and…was perfectly happy on the stage", when famous director John Ford approached Tracy and offered him a lead role in his next film, Tracy agreed to do a screen test. Ford's company, Fox Film Corporation, was not entirely pleased with Tracy's looks and stage presence, but fortunately, Ford had enough clout in Hollywood to get his way. Ford cast Tracy in *Up the River*, which premiered in 1930 and also starred Humphrey Bogart, and as soon as they saw Tracy's work, the Fox executives changed their minds about Tracy and offered him a contract. Needing the money to help care for his wife and deaf son, who had also contracted polio by now, Tracy signed the contract and thus moved his family to the West Coast.

John Ford

Chapter 4: Fledgling Hollywood Careers

"I strike people as peculiar in some way, although I don't quite understand why. Of course, I have an angular face, an angular body and, I suppose, an angular personality, which jabs into people." – Katharine Hepburn

"I've never known what acting is. Who can honestly say what it is? ... I wonder what actors are supposed to be, if not themselves ... I've finally narrowed it down to where, when I begin a part, I say to myself, this is Spencer Tracy as a judge, or this is Spencer Tracy as a priest or as a lawyer, and let it go at that. Look, the only thing an actor has to offer a director and finally an audience is his instinct. That's all." – Spencer Tracy

As Spencer Tracy and his family headed to California, the Fox Company was in its infancy and committed to growing as many stars as it could from its new finds. With that in mind, they supported Tracy all the way, giving him a significant role in the film *Quick Millions* in 1931 and arranging as many opportunities as possible for him to meet with the press. Even after *Quick Millions* did not do well, Fox still believed in Tracy and his talent and continued to give him roles in one movie after another. Nevertheless, none of these films did well, due more to the poor quality of the scripts and the filming than Tracy's acting ability, but it still looked like the actor might have to leave Hollywood and go back east to stage work.

With his career seemingly on the ropes, Tracy's seventh movie, *Disorderly Conduct*, became his most profitable movie since *Up the River*, but despite the popularity of his first and seventh full-length films, most of the public had not yet heard of Spencer Tracy. Dissatisfied with the quality of the roles he was being offered, Tracy threatened to leave Fox when his contract ran out in 1932, but the company still believed in him and wanted to recoup some of their investment. They offered to raise his salary to $1500 per week, but in spite of the money they were paying him, Fox continued to cast Tracy in what could most kindly be described as "B movies". He appeared in *Me and My Gal* in 1932 and later, while on loan to Warner Bros., in *20,000 Years in Sing Sing* with Bette Davis.

Spencer Tracy in *Disorderly Conduct*

Tracy finally received the professional attention he was craving when he starred as Tom Garner in *The Power and the Glory* in 1932. Written by Preston Sturges, *The Power and the Glory* tells the story of Garner's rise to power and wealth during the golden days of the railroad industry. Critics loved the film, with one effusing that "this sterling performer has finally been given an opportunity to show an ability that has been boxed in by gangster roles ... [the film] has introduced Mr. Tracy as one of the screen's best performers". Another critic added, "No more convincing performance has been given on the screen than Spencer Tracy's impersonation of Tom Garner." Tracy never considered himself a good-looking man, once commenting that his face was "as plain as a barn door" and wondering why people would "pay thirty-five cents to look at it", but he became more appealing in the movie *Shanghai Madness* in 1933.

Although *A Bill of Divorcement* (1932) did not achieve lasting fame, it was a fairly substantial film for Hepburn and RKO, which at the time was not one of the larger studios. Hepburn starred opposite John Barrymore, and the somewhat heavy-handed romantic plot featured Hepburn and Barrymore as Sydney and Hilary, who come together as a romantic couple despite the strong probability that any children they have will inherit the mental illness that runs throughout Hilary's family. The film performed strongly at the box office, and Katharine received rave reviews. *New York Times* critic Mordaunt Hall described her performance as "exceptionally fine... Miss Hepburn's characterization is one of the finest seen on the screen", and a review in the publication *The Variety* beamed, "Standout here is the smash impression made by Katharine Hepburn in her first picture assignment. She has a vital something that sets her apart from the picture galaxy." Naturally, RKO signed Hepburn to a long-term contract after the success and reviews.

Hepburn in *A Bill of Divorcement*

After Hepburn signed her long-term contract with RKO, she was relegated to the demanding work schedule characteristic of all studio actors who were not major stars. In 1933, she appeared in three films: *Christopher Strong*, *Morning Glory*, and *Little Women*. But these films launched Hepburn to the forefront of Hollywood; *Morning Glory* won her an Academy Award for Best Actress, while *Little Women* was one of RKO's most successful films and reunited Hepburn with George Cukor. Hepburn was especially proud of her work in *Little Women*, boasting, "I defy anyone to be as good as I was."

Hepburn in *Little Women*

Hepburn in *Morning Glory*

Katharine's cocksure attitude also manifested itself on sets. Instead of wearing traditional women's clothes, she preferred dressing comfortably, explaining in a later interview, "I wore pants when they weren't fashionable; I sat down on the curb if I was tired; I did what I wanted and what I thought was reasonable so long as I didn't hurt anyone. But is that so unusual?" At the same time, she helped design and pick out the elaborate costumes she wore in the films she was appearing in. Edith Head, who designed costumes for *The Rainmaker* (1956) and *Rooster Cogburn* (1975), explained, "One does not design for Miss Hepburn. One designs with her. She's a real professional, and she has very definite feelings about what things are right for her, whether it has to do with costumes, scripts, or her entire lifestyle." Hepburn stressed the importance of designing costumes, even as she downplayed the importance of clothes: "I take a tremendous amount of care over my costumes. I'll stand longer over a fitting than anybody. But you can't judge someone by what he's wearing. It's the inner part that counts."

The films were turning Hepburn into a star, but these early films also proved that RKO didn't quite know what to do with her, since there was very little continuity between the characters she played in the three films. Hepburn played a female aviatrix in *Christopher Strong*, a tomboy named Jo in *Little Women*, and a small town girl who rises to fame on Broadway in *Morning Glory*. Hepburn's unusual physical appearance made it difficult for the studio to cast her, as she did not cohere with the norms for a romantic lead during the time period (although she appeared in such a role in *Morning Glory*.) Furthermore, her physique also made her look especially youthful, leading to the kind of role she had in *Little Women*. While most actresses of her inexperience were typecast into relatively standard parts, Hepburn's unusual and unique appearance made it difficult to assign her to a particular "type" of role, as emphasized by the fact she was cast as a tomboy in one film and then as a romantic lead in the next. But ultimately, her unusual physique and raw, untrained acting style brought her into the public eye more rapidly than most actresses, even while making it more difficult to find parts that would accommodate such a singular presence.

Hepburn may have reached fame at an especially fast pace, but she fell out of public favor almost as quickly. At the end of 1933, Hepburn yearned to perform on Broadway once again, and she did so by appearing in *The Lake* (1933), directed by major theatrical producer Jed Harris. The play opened prematurely at Jed Harris' insistence, and an unprepared Hepburn was panned for her performance. The play had a formative impact on Hepburn; reflecting back on the experience, she noted, "I let Jed Harris, the producer, push me around. I knew that I was being pushed around and I didn't talk back. I didn't say, "Look, I am the one who has to sell this and if you make me into a mush, I'll just be a mush. And I was a mush." Given the strong personality she had exhibited from an early age, it is difficult to believe that Hepburn would have allowed herself to be taken advantage of in such a manner, but the episode does highlight the vulnerability that lurked beneath the veneer of the young Hepburn, the same vulnerability that had caused her to become reclusive at Bryn Mawr. Even though *The Lake* was an unmitigated disaster, the experience had the productive effect of clarifying the importance of working on her own terms.

From 1934-1938, Hepburn's performances were mostly criticized, and the films in which she appeared lost money. For this reason, she was famously labeled by the Independent Theatre Owners of America as "box office poison", but she still remained active during that time, appearing in 10 films with RKO: *Spitfire* (1934), *The Little Minister* (1934), *Break of Hearts* (1935), *Alice Adams* (1935), *Sylvia Scarlett* (1935), *Mary of Scotland* (1936), *A Woman Rebels* (1936), *Quality Street* (1937), *Stage Door* (1937), and *Bringing Up Baby* (1938). In truth, it is unfair to equate the poor box office showings of these films with poor performances from Hepburn, who in many cases was simply a victim of poor scripts and the changing preferences of the American public. What is true, however, is that Hepburn challenged audiences in a manner that made them uncomfortable. In *Sylvia Scarlett*, for example, Hepburn plays the eponymous role, in which she appears as a girl disguised as a boy. Her performance is quite convincing, yet the subversive, gender-bending nature of the role was discomforting to contemporary audiences and raised uncomfortable themes. Some even made the argument that Hepburn appeared more attractive in the film as a boy than as a girl, and 1930s audiences were unprepared for such motifs.

Hepburn in *Sylvia Scarlett*

One of the most significant developments that occurred during this period of box office failure was her friendship with Cary Grant, who was then still quite young himself. Grant and Hepburn appeared together in *Sylvia Scarlett*, and they would reunite to star together in *Bringing Up Baby* (1938). Despite performing somewhat poorly at the box office, *Bringing Up Baby* is now acclaimed as one of the most famous examples of the screwball comedy genre. The two stars played scientists dedicated to restoring dinosaur skeletons, and the narrative combines their developing romance with zany comedy. Hepburn proved to be an exceptional actress for the screwball genre; not only did the quirky plot suit her eccentric personality, but the strong female agency associated with the genre was commensurate with her personality as well. *Bringing Up Baby* is not only a humorous romantic film but an example of the potential for women to exist in marriage without succumbing to male-dominated conventions. In this regard, the film is subversive, even while it appears to be simply a lighthearted comedy.

Hepburn and Cary Grant in *Bringing Up Baby*

Given its current renown, it's difficult to believe that *Bringing Up Baby* could be anything other than a box office sensation, but there was a strong element of truth to the declaration that Hepburn was "box office poison." She alienated audiences with her very presence; at a time in which the country was in the throes of the Great Depression, the inflection of her voice exuded an elitist, snobbish tone. Moreover, the public was well-aware that Hepburn had come from a wealthy East Coast family, which only heightened the perceived pretentiousness of her performances onscreen. Realizing that they had an unmanageable star in their grasp, RKO was determined to provoke Hepburn into leaving, which they hoped to accomplish by casting her in a demeaning role in *Mother Carey's Chickens* (1938). After her humiliating experience working with Jed Harris, Hepburn was intent on not allowing herself to be deployed in such a manner, and later in 1938 she bought out her contract with RKO for $75,000. The move was unprecedented. In an era in which stars were essentially pawns to their governing studio, Hepburn was ahead of her time in asserting her independence, and she was now free to operate as an independent contractor for the remainder of her career.

While breaking away from the studio brought Hepburn great satisfaction and was an astute move for her career, the act was not perceived as such by the public at the time. She headed back to Fenwick, which the public viewed as an act of resignation regarding her film career, but Anne Edwards explained Hepburn's own attitude, "The Hollywood pundits wrongly believed

Katharine Hepburn had retreated to her family's summer cottage to nurse her wounds. Throughout May and June, the 'fallen' star was happier than she had been for years and was certain that in no time at all she would make those Hollywood dolts eat every last nasty word they had said of her."

The reasons for this public perception were understandable, since leaving RKO forfeited all the security Katharine had maintained while under the umbrella of the studio. However, back then, what a studio actress gained in protection she lost in freedom. Hepburn was now free to pursue any role she desired, regardless of the studio.

The same period of the time was turbulent for Tracy too. In the mid-1930s, he seemed to be on the verge of joining the ranks of premiere Hollywood leading men, but when a pair of movies failed to gain any serious attention in 1933, Tracy increasingly turned to the bottle for comfort. After a two week binge held up the filming of *Marie Galante* in 1934, Fox pulled him from acting and had him hospitalized for detox and treated for alcoholism. When Tracy was well enough to go to trial, they also sued him for the $125,000 they lost due to delays in filming. Needless to say, Tracy was not pleased at having to pay up, and he would only remain with Fox for two more pictures.

Tracy and Loretta Young in *Man's Castle* (1933)

Upon leaving Fox in April 1935, Tracy went to work at Metro-Goldwyn-Mayer, which was at that time looking for a new leading man. Given his reputation as a drunk who was hard to work with, it might seem surprising that MGM even hired Tracy, but critics loved him and MGM producer Irving G. Thalberg saw something in him that he believed he could make great. He insisted that MGM handle Tracy with kid gloves and went out of his way to cast him opposite of the best actresses of the day. Thus, during the mid-1930s, Tracy played in *Whipsaw* opposite of Myrna Loy and in *Riffraff* opposite of Jean Harlow. Neither of these films were very successful, and they actually had the backward effect of portraying Tracy as a hanger-on being carried by beautiful women.

This perception permanently changed in 1936 when Tracy starred in *Fury*, playing a man who is nearly hung by a lynch mob and then goes on to punish those who mistreated him so badly. This time, Tracy hit the jackpot. Not only was Fury popular with critics, the viewing public also loved it, so much so that Fury went on to make $1.3 million, a princely sum at the time. Tracy's biographer James Curtis explained the effect the movie had on Tracy's career, noting that "audiences who, just a year earlier, had no clear handle on him, were suddenly turning out to see him. It was a transition that was nothing short of miraculous...a willingness on the part of the public to embrace a leading man who was not textbook handsome nor bigger than life."

Just a month after *Fury* was released, Tracy's next movie, *San Francisco*, came out. In that movie, he starred with Clark Gable as a priest trying to help singer Mary Blake (played by Jeanette MacDonald), and even though he only had 17 minutes of screen time in the whole movie, his role was pivotal and powerful. In fact, the role was so powerful that it garnered Tracy his first Oscar nomination for Best Actor. *San Francisco* went on to be the biggest Hollywood moneymaker of 1936, leading biographer Donald Deschner to conclude *Fury* and *San Francisco* were the "two films that changed his career and gave him the status of a major star." Tracy's next picture, the screwball comedy *Libeled Lady*, was also a hit, making it his third in less than a year. Part of Tracy's success may have stemmed from the fact that he was "on the wagon" at the time, and without the complications of alcohol clouding his judgment, Tracy was able to focus more clearly on his roles and give them everything he had. This paid off, especially as he gained a new reputation as a professional actor who could be counted on.

During what is now known as the golden era of Hollywood, it was not uncommon for actors and actresses to film several movies every year, and this was as true for Spencer Tracy as it was anyone else. Even after the successes of 1936 (and no doubt due in part to them), in 1937 he appeared in four feature-length films. The first, entitled *They Gave Him a Gun*, was a box office failure, but his second film, *Captains Courageous*, is still considered a classic today. In the film, Tracy plays the captain of a poor Portuguese fishing boat that picks up the spoiled son of a wealthy tycoon. Ironically, the man who struggled being a father in real life did a remarkable job on screen becoming a father figure to the boy and introducing him to the rough-and-tumble life of 19th century manhood. Though Tracy resented having both his character's foreign accent and curly hair, he was great in the role and won the Oscar for Best Actor in 1937, even though he not there to receive it. As he humorously explained in an interview:

"I knew I was going to lose. Three of the five were Metro: Bob and Bowyer and me. So the studio couldn't very well campaign for one of us or pass the word without getting a million-dollar beef from somebody. They were boxed in. Warners was pushing you the hard; and, of course, Selznick was all out for Freddie. And remember that not only was Selznick the greatest operator in the history of Hollywood, but in this case he had what most people including me thought was the best performance to plunk for. God damn, that Freddie was good. Anyway I don't have to tell you… I may be a long about some things but not about acting. I know I'm pretty good, and in *Captains* I was a little better, maybe Barry. I mean, I'm a good actor, but I'm a son of a bitch if I thought I had an expression in my box to put on my face when they announced the winner, Frederick Mark and sitting there in soup and fish, to top it off. And I sure didn't want to reach for the kind of liquid help I was going to need to get through anything like that not in that particular group. So…It was a situation. The studio was insisting I show there was going to be hell to pay if I didn't. Finally I got an idea. Dr. Dennis you know Howard was not only my doctor, he was my friend. And I went to him and laid it on the line. I told him I couldn't go through with it. So he said, quote 'well, what you want me to do? Pick it up for you and make a speech?' And I said, 'No, Denny, but you know my hernia….' Well what can I tell you? Denny was a friend, and he shot me into the hospital and I didn't have to go to the Academy's god damn banquet. Of course, I did have to have the operation. And you can imagine what I felt like lying there, and all those itchy bandages around my middle, and plenty of pain when the word came through, I'd won it?"

Tracy in Captains Courageous

Fortunately, Tracy wouldn't have to wait long to get another chance to accept an Oscar. Based on his rapport with young Freddie Bartholomew in *Captains Courageous*, Tracy was cast as the famous founder of Boys Town, Father Edward J. Flanagan, in the movie *Boys Town*. The role made him so nervous that he admitted, "I'm so anxious to do a good job as Father Flanagan that it worries me, keeps me awake at night." Ultimately, Tracy did an excellent job and the movie was another box office smash, resulting in yet another Oscar nomination in 1938. When he won it that year, he became one of the only actors to ever receive two Academy Awards for Best Actor in a row. This time, he explained how he got ready for winning the award:

> "When I got the one for Boys Town, I got up and made my speech and I don't

remember the words exactly but something to the effect that I didn't deserve it, that it belonged to Father Flanagan and that all I'd done was let his light shine through me and so I wanted to thank him for the privilege of impersonating him and accepting the award for him. Something like that. And I sat down. In those days used to go back to your seat after getting it. I guess I must've overdone it a little, because Frank Morgan was sitting right behind me, and he leaned forward and whispered, 'I didn't see you in the picture, Spence, but you sure deserve that statue for the performance you just gave up there!'"

The next day, Tracy sent the statuette itself to Flanagan.

In many ways, Tracy always had a problem reconciling his love for the church and his love for acting, sex and liquor. He once confessed to a friend that he thought he might have missed his true calling, saying, "Every time I play a priest, and I've done my share, Father Flanagan in those two *Boys Town* ones and Father Mullin in *San Francisco* and Father Doing in *The Devil at 4 o'clock* every time I put on the clothes and the collar I feel right, right away. Like they were mine, like I belonged in them, and that feeling of being, what's the word, an intermediary is always very appealing those were always my most comfortable parts...."

After his experience of filming four films in one year, Tracy understandably decided to take a year off, and he did not return to the big screen again until 1939, when he starred as Henry M. Stanley in *Stanley and Livingstone*. Apparently, his absence only made the hearts of his fan grow fonder, because the survey in October of that year found Tracy to be the most popular movie actor in America.

Though Tracy was very popular with his audience, he was not so well loved within the confines of his own home. After years of conflict going back to the birth of their first son, Spencer and Louise Tracy separated in 1933. Unlike many stars at that time, Tracy was open about his marital problems, and he and Louise both told the press that they had no intention to divorce but would remain separated. For the next year, Tracy had an affair with Loretta Young, whom he had met while filming *Man's Castle*, but in 1935, he broke off his relationship with Young and returned home to Louise and his children. While they would never separate again, they wouldn't live together as man and wife in the traditional sense either. By the early 1940s, Tracy was no longer living at home, instead preferring to stay in various hotels and the beds of various actresses that he met while filming. He is alleged to have had affairs with Joan Crawford in 1937 and Ingrid Bergman in 1941.

Chapter 5: Tracy and Hepburn

"I'm a personality as well as an actress. Show me an actress who isn't a personality and you'll show me a woman who isn't a star." – Katharine Hepburn

"I can get a divorce whenever I want to. But my wife and Kate like things just as they are." – Spencer Tracy

After breaking away from RKO, Hepburn had no obstructions preventing her from working with Cary Grant and George Cukor, her favorite co-star and director at the time. Moreover, there was a script that was tailor-made for her: a remake of the 1930 film *Holiday*. With Grant, Cukor, and Hepburn signing on to appear in the film, Columbia Pictures agreed to release the film in June 1938. The film, another screwball comedy, featured Hepburn and Grant involved in a romance against the best wishes of Hepburn's stern, old-money father.

It's impossible not to notice the semi-autobiographical elements at work in the film. Hepburn's portrayal of an eccentric from a wealthy family was clearly in line with her background, even if her parents were far more liberal than her parents in the film. Hepburn appears as a fun, quirky figure with easy appeal to present-day audiences, and in this regard *Holiday* should have marked Hepburn's return to public favor. However, *Holiday* is yet another example of why it's important to evaluate films based on the context in which they were made. Contemporary audiences had great difficulty identifying with wealthy characters, and the anxieties of the rich were of little concern to viewers who struggled to come up with money to even attend the film they were watching. In an era in which Frank Capra and John Ford directed socially-aware films like *Mr. Smith Goes to Washington* (1939) and *The Grapes of Wrath* (1940), *Holiday* failed to exhibit the kind of concern for the struggling common man that was needed during the time period. *Holiday* is a film that likely would have achieved greater success had it been produced in a different era. The next film that Hepburn acted in would make her a smaller salary than she had made for her first film, and as writer Andrew Britton aptly put it, "No other star has emerged with greater rapidity or with more ecstatic acclaim. No other star, either, has become so unpopular so quickly for so long a time."

Hepburn and Grant in *Holiday*

Holiday may not have marked the return to commercial success that Hepburn had desired, but the film did not deter her from reuniting with Grant and Cukor either, and the trio would work together on what would arguably become Hepburn's most famous film, *The Philadelphia Story* (1940), which was turned into a film after Hepburn starred in a successful tour of it on the stage. Hepburn was sensitive of the need to appear in a more humble role, and this semi-autobiographical play and film cast her as Tracy Lord, an extremely wealthy socialite who is caught choosing between the rich C.K. Dexter Haven (played in the film by Cary Grant) and the more humble Mike Connor (played in the film by James Stewart). Much of the film's entertainment derives from the unpredictability of choosing between the two male leads, especially since there were arguably no more popular actors than Cary Grant and James Stewart in 1940. In the end, Hepburn selects Stewart, a move that endeared her to the still-financially strapped American public. The film was an immense success, grossing roughly $3 million in revenue.

Hepburn later explained that by playing Tracy Lord, ""I gave her life and she gave me back my career." There's no doubt that Hepburn recognized the ability of the role to shape her public image, and she configured parts of the film to ensure that audiences would view Tracy Lord as a sympathetic figure. During the filming, she noted, "I don't want to make a grand entrance in this picture. Moviegoers ... think I'm too la-di-da or something. A lot of people want to see me fall flat on my face." The idea was to have the audience "laugh at her enough that they would ultimately sympathize with her." In that vein, it was a wild success, and that theme was even echoed in a review that appeared in *Time*, which stated, "Come on back, Katie, all is forgiven."

Hepburn did indeed improve her public standing with *The Philadelphia Story*, but the film is progressive from a gender standpoint. Even though it was produced while Hepburn was still at the nadir of her popularity, she still appears as a remarkably strong woman, and in an era in which leading roles for women were rare, Hepburn is not only the main character but also endowed with the authority to select the man she marries. The film succeeded in portraying Hepburn in a more humble role, yet she is also arguably never more powerful than in this film. In reference to this dynamic, Andrew Britton argued, "While we are invited, at the end of *The Philadelphia Story*, to take comfort in the discovery of Tracy Lord (Katharine Hepburn) that 'men are wonderful' as a satisfactory resolution of the problems of the film, we have also previously been allowed to celebrate those very qualities which must be humbled to engineer this 'happy ending'. The contradiction—which embodies a conflict both of values and of possibilities of pleasure—is insoluble."

Thus, even as the film superficially subscribes to the traditional images of marriage, Hepburn dominates the relationship in a manner that suggests female dominance at the same time. As a result, *The Philadelphia Story* accomplished the twin tasks of restoring Hepburn's popularity and doing so in a manner that retained her individuality.

Hepburn and James Stewart in *The Philadelphia Story*

While Hepburn was resurrecting his career, Tracy followed up his year-long break and returned to moviemaking with a vengeance, making another four movies in 1940. The first, *I Take this Woman*, did not do well, but *The Northwest Passage*, his first color movie, was very popular. Continuing with this historical theme, Tracy played Thomas Edison in the movie *Edison, The Man*, and though the movie itself was not considered very good, critics continue to be impressed by Tracy's acting. Tracy's fourth movie of 1940, *Boomtown*, starred Clark Gable and Claudette Colbert, as well as Heddy Lamar. The media frenzy leading up to the movie was tremendous, and its opening crowd rivaled that of *Gone With the Wind*.

In the spring of 1941, MGM gave Tracy a new contract that paid him $5000 a week and expressly stated he would not be required to make more than three pictures a year. From this point forward, he would not only be listed as the star of every movie that he appeared in but also almost always have top billing. A few months later, MGM, always happy to make use of a good idea by releasing a sequel to *Boys Town* called *A Man at Boys Town*, but it was something of a box office failure. Next, Tracy tried his hand at playing the title role in *Dr. Jekyll and Mr. Hyde*, and even though he was never crazy about his face, he preferred showing it to the screen naturally rather than being made up in the heavy theatrical makeup that he was forced to wear as Mr. Hyde. Lawrence Olivier once teased him for not liking stage makeup, saying "I admire so much about you, Spence, but nothing more than the fact that you can do it all they are faced." When Olivier asked Tracy if he felt naked without makeup, Tracy replied, "Only when I have to say a lousy line."

In 1941, Tracy and Hepburn began filming *Woman of the Year*, a film that would mark the beginning of one of the most famous off-screen and on-screen love affairs in Hollywood history. As one of Hollywood's most popular actresses at the time, and fresh off the success of *The Philadelphia Story*, Katharine Hepburn was allowed to select the director and co-star of her choice for *Woman of the Year*, and she chose George Stevens as director and Tracy as the leading man. The film featured Hepburn and Tracy as newspaper journalists engaged in a battle of the sexes that evolves into romance. Although the film's title and plot are progressive insofar as Hepburn appears as a career woman, it was less progressive than *The Philadelphia Story*. While that has led some critics to criticize *Woman of the Year* for the gender politics at work, the film's treatment of gender is no different from that of the subsequent films Hepburn appeared in with Tracy. Much of this dynamic is simply due to the image of the short and stout Tracy, whose figure embodied patriarchy.

Regardless of the actual roles the two stars played, Hepburn was determined not to be intimidated by her leading man. Since she was rather tall and knew that Tracy was only a little over 5'10, Hepburn showed up at their meeting wearing some of her highest heeled shoes. The film opened to rave reviews, and one critic summed the situation up: "To begin with, it has Katharine Hepburn and Spencer Tracy in the leading roles. This in itself would be enough to make any film memorable. But when you get Tracy and Hepburn turning in brilliant performances to boot, you've got something to cheer about." Other critics agreed, with one writing, "Her performance is a constant pleasure to watch. Mr. Tracy is an excellent foil for her in this particular instance. His quiet, masculine stubbornness and prosaic outlook on life is in striking contrast to her startling brilliance. They make a fine team, and each complements the other." Another reviewer, James Agee, writing for *Time*, noted, "Actors Hepburn and Tracy have a fine time in Woman of the Year. They take turns playing straight for each other, act one superbly directed love scene, and succeed in turning several batches of cinematic corn into passable moonshine. As a lady columnist, she's just right. As a working reporter, he is practically perfect. For once, striding Katharine Hepburn is properly subdued."

Hepburn in *Woman of the Year*

These comments, and many more, would come to apply to the two in real life as well as in their films. The unmarried Hepburn soon fell in love with Tracy, and he with her. The relationship was surprising on many levels. Tracy was already married, and due to religious beliefs, he was unwilling to receive a divorce. And while he was only 7 years older than Hepburn, his soft features and wrinkled face made him appear much older than her as well. It's somewhat surprising that Hepburn would embark on another relationship with an older man after previous relationships with older men didn't turn out well, but even though they never married, Tracy and Hepburn would remain committed to each other with unwavering mutual devotion, not only off the set but in films as well. In fact, it's possible that the lack of an actual marriage appealed to Hepburn, who by this time had not only turned down Leland Hayward but also the eccentric Howard Hughes, whom she had also dated. At the same time, Tracy wasn't any more faithful to Hepburn than he had been to his wife. He continued to engage in romantic affairs, including one with Gene Tierney, whom he met while filming *Plymouth Adventure*.

Perhaps one of the strengths of Spencer Tracy's relationship with Katharine Hepburn was that he treated her like a lady and also considered her his equal in every way. This applied even in cases where it didn't seem to matter very much. For instance, one writer took him to task for being billed above Hepburn on movie posters, saying "Well, after all, she's the lady. You're the man. Ladies first?" To which Tracy replied, "This is a movie, chowder head, not a lifeboat." Meanwhile, unlike Tracy, who prided himself on the ease with which he appeared on stage, Hepburn took her acting career very seriously. This led to some interesting discussions between the two, including one time when Hepburn asked Tracy in front of friends what he felt the secret to acting to be. Looking at them wryly, he said, "Well, it's taken me 40 years of doing it to learn the secret. I don't know that I want to give it away." They insisted, and he finally replied, "Okay, I'll tell you. The art of acting is: LEARN YOUR LINES!" With that, he left the room.

It is at least conceivable that Tracy and Hepburn would not have gotten away with such torrid adultery given the era, but their screen presence was so powerful that MGM was more than willing to help protect their mutual reputations. While their relationship was an open secret in Hollywood, few outside the city knew about it until near the end of Tracy's life. Over the next three decades, the two would make nine movies together, all of them box office hits.

As soon as he finished *Woman of the Year*, Tracy began work on *Turkey Flat*, but even his star power could not save that movie. However, as that film was falling flat, *Woman of the Year* was a smash hit, so MGM cast Tracy and Hepburn together again in *Keeper of the Flame*. Unlike the comedic *Woman of the Year*, *Keeper of the Flame* was a dramatic mystery, and even though the critics did not care for it, the public loved it enough that the film made even more money than *Woman of the Year* had.

By this time, the United States was firmly ensconced in World War II and Hollywood was doing its part, so it was only natural that Tracy's next three movies were about war. The first, entitled *A Guy Named Joe*, became his most popular movie to date, while the next, *The Seventh Cross* (1944), told a harrowing story of an escape from a concentration camp. Tracy's third war picture, *30 Seconds over Tokyo*, was about American bombers running campaigns over Tokyo. The combined receipts of these three movies made Spencer Tracy MGM's most profitable star of 1944.

Exhausted from three movies in 12 months, Tracy again took a year off, returning in 1945 to again star with Hepburn, this time in *Without Love*. Though the usual chemistry between the two actors was there, and the viewing public responded well, the critics panned the movie, declaring it not up to Tracy's usual standards. At this point, Tracy took a short time off from making movies to return to Broadway in a play called *The Rugged Path*, written by Robert E Sherwood. Unfortunately, producing the show proved to be more challenging than anyone had anticipated, as the director later recalled, "In the ten days prior to the New York opening all the important relationships had deteriorated. Spencer was tense and unbending, could not, or would not, take direction". The production only ran for 81 performances before Tracy quit, saying, "I couldn't say those goddamn lines over and over and over again every night ... At least every day is a new day for me in films ... But this thing—every day, every day, over and over again." As that quote would suggest, *The Rugged Path* was the last play for the actor who had once loved the stage so much that he was reluctant to act in films.

After that last stint on Broadway, Tracy returned to Hollywood and Hepburn in *The Sea of Grass*, a classic Western released in 1947. Yet again, the critics were not crazy about their work together but the public loved them. Tracy followed *The Sea of Grass* with *Cass Timberlane*, which also starred Lana Turner.

Tracy in *The Sea of Grass*

In 1948, Frank Capra asked Tracy and Hepburn to star in *The State of the Union*, which has Tracy playing a presidential candidate who is pressured to adopt a platform supporting big business. Hepburn plays his estranged wife, who reemerges and steers him toward a more socially-committed platform. The film marked just how far Hepburn had transformed from the early roles that had marked her as pretentious. Hepburn had always been liberal, but with films such as *State of the Union*, she exuded a concern for the working class, and the fact that she appeared in a Frank Capra film demonstrated her turn toward a more socially compassionate identity.

Hepburn and Tracy in *Adam's Rib*

The following year, in 1949, Tracy appeared as the villain in *Edward My Son*. The director, George Cooper, was surprised that Tracy did not like the part and was even more disappointed when critics criticized him for miscasting Tracy in the role. Always the professional, Tracy admitted, "It's rather disconcerting to me to find how easily I play a heel." However, *Edward My Son* would be one of Tracy's worst films and one of the few he ever made for MGM that actually lost money.

After Tracy starred with Jimmy Stewart in a World War II themed movie, *Malaya*, he returned to his bread-and-butter: the screwball comedy *Adam's Rib*. Once again, he starred with Katherine Hepburn as married lawyers who oppose each other in court. Hepburn displays a concern for social welfare while she defends a woman who murdered her husband in self-defense, but after defeating Tracy in court she resumes her marriage as though nothing had happened. The film is another example of how Hepburn portrayed career women but did so within the confines of traditional gender relations and marriage.

As the description of the roles suggests, the roles were written specifically for Tracy and Hepburn, whose energy together was infectious and magical. *Adam's Rib* remains a popular comedy today, and one reviewer aptly described their chemistry together: "As we say, Mr. Tracy and Miss Hepburn are the stellar performers in this show and their perfect compatibility in comic capers is delightful to see. A line thrown away, a lifted eyebrow, a smile or a sharp, resounding slap on a tender part of the anatomy is as natural as breathing to them. Plainly, they took great pleasure in playing this rambunctious spoof."

Chapter 6: The 1950s and 60s

"The kids keep telling me I should try this new 'Method Acting' but I'm too old, I'm too tired and I'm too talented to care." – Spencer Tracy

"I'm disappointed in acting as a craft. I want everything to go back to Orson Welles and fake noses and changing your voice. It's become so much about personality." – Spencer Tracy

At the close of the '40s, Hollywood became an increasingly tumultuous environment, thanks to the Red Scare. After World War II, the burgeoning Cold War between the West and the Soviet Union stirred hysteria across the United States. Though anti-Communist sentiment in the 1950s is often derisively dismissed as McCarthyism, there was some basis for the era's fears, since the Communist Party in the United States was funded by the Soviet Union, and several were agents of the Soviet intelligence apparatus. But the real threat was exaggerated to a degree that comes across as completely farcical today. Shortly after World War II, Congress' House Committee on Un-American Activities began investigating Americans across the country for suspected ties to Communism, and U.S. Senator Joseph McCarthy made waves in 1950 by telling the Republican Women's Club in Wheeling, West Virginia that he had a list of dozens of known Communists working in the State Department. The political theater helped Senator McCarthy become the prominent anti-Communist crusader in the government, and the Rosenberg spy case only further emboldened him. McCarthy continued to claim he held evidence suggesting Communist infiltration throughout the government, but anytime he was pressed to produce his evidence, McCarthy would not name names. Instead, he'd accuse those who questioned his evidence of being Communists themselves.

The most famous victims of these witch hunts were Hollywood actors, such as Charlie Chaplin, whose "Un-American activity" was being neutral at the beginning of World War II. When 10 Hollywood members refused to appear before the Committee to testify, they were cited for contempt of Congress and blacklisted. Although Hepburn was never called to testify before the House Un-American Activities Committee, she was unwavering and outspoken in her liberal views, which hurt her public image. While denying she was a Communist or sympathized with them, she nevertheless stated, "I always just say be on the affirmative and liberal side. Don't be a 'no' person."

Distancing herself from Hollywood and the chaos swirling around it, Hepburn returned to the stage during the 1950s and appeared in a number of Shakespeare productions. The first of these was *As You Like It* (1950), and subsequent performances in Shakespeare plays included *The Taming of the Shrew* (1955), *The Merchant of Venice* (1955), *Measure for Measure* (1955), *Much Ado About Nothing* (1957), *Twelfth Night* (1960), and *Antony and Cleopatra* (1960).

Aside from the opportunity to return to the medium in which she began, there were logistical advantages to working in theater. Hepburn owned an apartment in New York City, and the East Coast location allowed her to oscillate conveniently between New York City and Fenwick. Her mother died in 1951, and living on the East Coast let her care for her father.

However, theater never supplanted Hepburn's work in film, and she returned to the cinema in 1951 for *The African Queen*. By the time shooting began for *The African Queen*, it had been nearly two years since she had appeared in a film, and she was already approaching her mid-40s, a time in which most stars began having difficulty securing leading roles. The plot involved sinking a German gunboat on the rivers of German-controlled East Africa during World War I. Humphrey Bogart plays Canadian Charlie Allnut, while Hepburn's character is Rose Sayer, a British missionary. Over the course of the film, they become romantic while also managing to sink the German boat through a plot engineered by Rose.

By collectively sinking the German boat, the film displays the romantic belief that love between two people can solve any obstacle. Hepburn and Bogart were an interesting pairing too, since she had spent much of her career appearing in screwball comedy films and he had acted in gangster films. They were thus equals and opposites at the same time, two individuals who finally united at a time in which they were beginning to grow old in front of the camera. Consequently, *The African Queen* contains an unusual balance between being an action film on the one hand (shot on location in Africa), while also a sentimental romance between two aging stars.

The African Queen marked a comeback film for Hepburn, and the production experience was by far the most ambitious of her career. The film was shot on the Congo River, and Hepburn became violently ill, losing a significant amount of weight and at one point finding herself in critical condition.

Hepburn and Bogart in *The African Queen*

The African Queen was significant not only for reigniting Hepburn's film career but also improving her image yet again in the eyes of the public. To this end, William Mann notes that while *The African Queen* is an adventure film with a great plot, it performed a necessary function in resurrecting Hepburn's public name: "Yet look closely and the various wanderings of her career take on new meaning. *The African Queen* becomes not just a chance great script but a deliberate stab at rehabilitation by Hepburn, Humphrey Bogart, and John Huston, all of whom had been painted Red by Communist witch-hunters just a year before. Hepburn the traitor was supplanted by Hepburn the Patriot, who sails down a muddy river enduring hardships for her country."

Mann is perhaps hyperbolic in proclaiming that Hepburn was intentionally capitalizing on the patriotism of the plot. Whether or not she was aware of the significance of the patriotic connotations of the script, however, *The African Queen* was a major commercial and critical success, and Hepburn's performance is still recognized as one of her greatest achievements.

For all of the acclaim bestowed upon Hepburn for *The African Queen*, the film is ideologically conservative and marked a less flattering development in the Hepburn image. She had previously played strong, career-driven women, but in *The African Queen* and subsequent films, Hepburn was relegated to portraying spinsters or passive married women, with the notable exception of *Pat and Mike* (1952) and a select few other films. In addition, Bogart's traditionally masculine image was similar to that of Spencer Tracy, reflecting how as Hepburn grew in age, she was frequently cast alongside icons of masculinity. The more conservative gender politics of such films marked a drastic change from Hepburn's early roles, even if they also came with critical and commercial acclaim.

By 1950, Spencer Tracy was 50 years old, and based on the standards of that time in

Hollywood, a middle-aged man was more suited to play father figure roles than that of virile leading men. One of his first roles of this kind was also one of his most famous. Tracy played Stanley Banks in *Father of the Bride*, a comedy in which he plays the father of bride Elizabeth Taylor and captures on-screen the role of every man who has ever tried to survive planning and paying for a wedding. While the movie was more of a vehicle for Taylor, audiences and critics alike praised Tracy's performance. *Father of the Bride* is still regularly seen on classic movie channels, his performance garnered him yet another Oscar nomination for Best Actor, and the movie earned more money than any other of his films to date. Along with the sequel, *Father's Little Dividend* (released the following year), *Father of the Bride* again propelled Tracy to the top of Hollywood's list of male actors.

Tracy and Taylor in *Father of the Bride*

After starring as a lawyer in *The People against O'Hara* in 1951, Tracy joined Hepburn to make *Pat and Mike* in 1952. Written for them by the same writers who developed *Adam's Rib*, Pat and Mike became the pair's most popular movie ever, with critics and viewers alike praising its charm and comedic timing. By then, Tracy was in his early 50s and Hepburn was 45, and they arguably looked even older than that, so the film might have been more appropriate if filmed earlier in their careers.

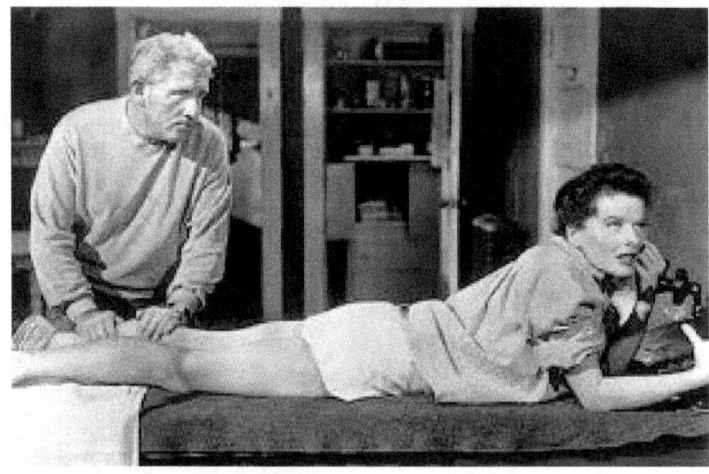

Hepburn and Tracy in *Pat and Mike*

Later that year, Tracy starred with Gene Tierney in *Plymouth Adventure*, another historical drama in the spirit of *Captains Courageous*, but *Plymouth Adventure* lacked the charm and quality writing of Courageous and fell flat at the box office. Tracy won his first Golden Globe award and earned a nomination for the British Academy Film and Theatre Award (BAFTA) for his next role, this time as a father in *The Actress*, but the critically acclaimed movie was a complete dud at the box office, with the producer lamenting "that film ... got more [acclaim] from the critics than any film I ever made in all the years, and we didn't make enough to pay for the ushers in the theatre."

Tracy returned to Westerns in 1954, starring in the film *Broken Lance* for 20th Century Fox and then appearing in a 1955 Western, *Bad Day at Black Rock*, as the one-armed misfit in a small western town. This role earned him the best actor prize at the Cannes Film Festival, but a few months later he was forced to quit in the middle of *Tribute to a Bad Man* because the altitude in Colorado, where they were shooting, made him sick. Tracy faced altitude sickness again in 1956 while filming *The Mountain* in the French Alps, but this time he was able to soldier through and completed the project. By that point, Tracy had left MGM for good, and he would remain an independent actor for the rest of his life.

Upon returning to America, Tracy also returned to Hepburn and a new comedy they filmed together called *Desk Set*. Even though he always loved working with Hepburn, Tracy was becoming increasingly undependable and almost did not complete the film. His lack of enthusiasm showed on-screen as well, and Desk Set became the least popular of the movies that he made with Hepburn.

Tracy and Hepburn in a publicity image for the 1957 film *Desk Set*.

In 1957, Tracy began work on *The Old Man and the Sea*, and unlike his recent roles, Tracy was enthusiastic about this film. However, his weight was considered a drawback in his portrayal of a rugged fisherman, and when he was urged to go on a diet in preparation for shooting, he refused to do so. He later described the movie as the most difficult he ever filmed, primarily because he had built his career around reacting to others on stage but appeared in most of the scenes alone in this film, but his acting was still superb enough to receive an Oscar nomination and a nomination for the British Academy Film Award. Reviewer Jack Moffitt wrote of Tracy's performance that it was "so intimate and revealing of universal human experience that, to me, it almost transcended acting and became reality."

28 years after filming their last movie together, Tracy reunited with director John Ford to make

The Last Hurrah in 1958, in which Tracy played an Irish-American hoping to be reelected mayor. While the National Board of Review chose Tracy as 1958's best actor, *The Last Hurrah* was something of a box office failure. Now 60 years old and looking even older than that, Tracy began to wonder if it was time for him to retire, but then came the opportunity to play Clarence Darrow in the famous movie *Inherit the Wind*. Based on the famous 1925 Scopes monkey trial, *Inherit the Wind* pitted Tracy's Clarence Darrow against William Jennings Bryan (played by Frederick Mark), and the film is now considered a classic and some of Tracy's best work. He received nominations for an Oscar and a Golden Globe award, but the public did not care as much for the movie, possibly due to the cultural sensitivity over the subject matter at the time.

Tracy in *Inherit the Wind*

The remaining films in which Hepburn appeared during the decade achieved varying degrees of success: *Summertime* (1955), *Desk Set* (1957), and *Suddenly, Last Summer* (1959). The most significant among these is probably *Summertime*, which was directed by David Lean, the famous British director who would later direct *Lawrence of Arabia* (1962) and *The Bridge on the River Kwai* (1957). Hepburn was quite fond of *Summertime*, in large part because she appreciated Lean's talents as a director. The film continued the theme of Hepburn as spinster, in which she portrays an elementary school secretary who spends her summer vacation in Venice, where she falls in love with a Venetian man. *Summertime* contains a number of scenic images of Venice, but the plot is relatively unremarkable.

By the beginning of the 1960s, Hepburn's productivity slowed considerably, as she averaged only one film every two to three years. This development was attributable to her appearing in more plays, as well as the fact that she spent so much personal time caring for Tracy and her father. Following the death of Katharine's mother in 1951, Tom had married one of his nurses, but Katharine still devoted a great deal of effort to looking after her father. His death in 1962 had a profound impact on her, and it would be compounded by Tracy's physical deterioration around the same time.

Tracy donned a Roman collar one last time in 1961 to play a priest in *The Devil at 4 O'Clock*. At first it looked like he might have to drop out of this picture because of some conflicts in his other filming schedule for *Judgment at Nuremburg*, but his costar Frank Sinatra and *Judgment*'s director, Stanly Kramer, were able to work things out so that Tracy could finish the film. While the critics did not love *The Devil at 4 O'Clock*, the public did, and it proved to be the most profitable film of the last decade of his career.

On the other hand, 1961's *Judgment at Nuremburg* is considered one of the best movies of the decade. The movie tells the story of the trials held for Nazi war criminals at the end of World War II, and the author, Anna Mann, wrote the character of Judge Haywood specifically for Tracy. For his part, Tracy said that it was the best script he ever read, and the film culminates in a 13 minute speech delivered by Tracy from the bench. Much to everyone's surprise, the 61-year-old actor nailed the entire speech in one take, earning an ovation from everyone on set after the scene was finished. Mann later wrote in a letter, "Every writer ought to have the experience of having Spencer Tracy do his lines. There is nothing in the world quite like it."

Due to his work on *Judgment at Nuremberg*, Tracy was not able to complete his role in *How the West Was Won*, but that movie's director, John Ford, was satisfied when Tracy agreed to do the narration for the film. By now in poor health, Tracy summoned his energy for one more film with Stanley Kramer, *A Mad, Mad, Mad, Mad World*, which became a '60s classic. Tracy only had a small role, but it required all his personal and professional energy to complete his role in just nine days, and the film went on to be the most profitable film of that year.

By the time *Its A Mad, Mad, Mad, Mad World* was finished, it seemed likely that Tracy would never act again, and indeed, he turned down one film after another, preferring to live quietly in a small house he shared with Katherine Hepburn. Despite being just 62 years old, Tracy had developed a severe heart disease, exacerbated by his bouts of alcoholism, and Hepburn moved in with him in his Beverley Hills apartment to provide constant nursing care. From the end of 1962 until 1967, Hepburn appeared in no films and devoted herself exclusively to caring for Tracy, but early in 1962 she appeared in what she would later consider one of her finest performances. In the stage adaptation of Eugene O'Neill's *Long Day's Journey into Night* (1962), Hepburn played matriarch Mary Tyrone, who is addicted to morphine and surrounded by a family of alcoholics. Hepburn delivers a bravura performance complete with wild histrionics, but the film is not particularly cinematic and comes across almost as a filmed theatrical production. In this regard, *Long Day's Journey into Night* is an example of how Hepburn's late career effectively synthesized theater and film (*Suddenly, Last Summer* is an even earlier example of this tendency.) While the 1950s had involved a clear divide between her film roles and her stage performances, the 1960s began blurring the line between the two, with many of her films from that point forward resonating as filmed adaptations of theatrical texts.

Hepburn in *Long Day's Journey into Night*

In 1967, Tracy agreed to star as the father in Stanly Kramer's *Guess Who's Coming To Dinner*. The film, which paired Tracy and Hepburn for the last time, was directed by Stanley Kramer and co-starred Sidney Poitier and Katharine Houghton, Hepburn's niece. The film is notable not only for being the final collaboration between Tracy and Hepburn but also because of its sensitive treatment of the still-controversial topic of interracial marriage. Tracy had once joked that "the physical labor actors have to do wouldn't tax an embryo", but by this point, Tracy's poor health meant he was only able to work only two or three hours each day, and he filmed his last scene on May 24, 1967.

Tracy in *Guess Who's Coming to Dinner*

Hepburn in *Guess Who's Coming to Dinner*

When *Guess Who's Coming To Dinner* was released later that December, it garnered Tracy the rare posthumous Oscar nomination for Best Actor. Just 17 days after filming his final scene, Tracy got out of bed early on June 10 and made his way to the kitchen for a cup of tea. Hearing him get up, Hepburn followed him into the kitchen, and as she later explained, "Just as I was about to give [the door] a push, there was a sound of a cup smashing to the floor—then clump— a loud clump." Spencer Tracy had suffered a sudden heart attack and was dead before his body hit the ground. As she rushed to his side, Hepburn recalled, "He looked so happy to be done with living, which for all his accomplishments had been a frightful burden for him."

The Tracy family planned an elaborate Requiem Mass for Spencer for June 12 that was held at Immaculate Heart of Mary Catholic Church in East Hollywood. Directors, actors, and other famous contemporaries showed up, and the only person dear to Tracy who was not there was Katherine Hepburn. Always the lady, she stayed away out of respect for Louise Tracy and her children. After the mass, Spencer Tracy was buried at the Forest Lawn Memorial Park in Glendale, California.

Many actors through the years have succumbed to being typecast and/or letting their personal lives so influence the parts that they played that they always seemed to be playing themselves. This was even truer during Hollywood's Golden Era, when every audience knew John Wayne's character would be a tough cowboy and Mae West would play a "bad woman" with a good heart. However, no one could ever accuse Spencer Tracy of having a type. After all, he might be a priest in one picture and a drunken bum in the next. He played famous lawyers and death row inmates with equal passion.

His roles did not seemingly reflect his personal life, but anyone who took a closer look would find that Tracy himself lived a life that was just as diverse as the parts he played. He could be a raging alcoholic but always remained a gentle man. He loved his wife too much to divorce her but not enough to live with her. His long affair with Katherine Hepburn is the stuff of legends, but he cheated on her too. In short, his life was a series of inconsistencies that went all the way back to the very beginning.

Chapter 7: Hepburn's Late Career

"I have no fear of death. Must be wonderful, like a long sleep." – Katharine Hepburn

After Tracy's death, Hepburn was suddenly alone at the age of 62, but instead of following in her father's footsteps and marrying late in life, she remained single. For companionship, she relied on her nurse, Phyllis Wilbourn. Although Hepburn has long been suspected of being bisexual throughout her entire life, the relationship with Wilbourn is believed to be strictly platonic by most biographers. Now that she was no longer tied to Tracy, Hepburn resumed spending much of her time on the East Coast, shifting between California, New York, and Fenwick. Although Tracy was the love of her life, her life following his death restored her independence and is representative of the strong persona that first made her famous.

Hepburn remained quite busy late in life. Immediately after Tracy's death, she appeared in *The Lion in Winter* (1968), in which she played the role of Eleanor of Aquitane and starred alongside Peter O'Toole and Anthony Hopkins. Although *The Lion in Winter* did not achieve the box office success of *Guess Who's Coming to Dinner*, it was still immensely popular and earned more than $20 million at the box office. The film was also the first in a string of period films for Hepburn that included *The Madwoman of Challot* (1969) and *The Trojan Woman* (1971).

Although she was relatively well-suited for her role in *The Lion in Winter*, the nature of her image clashed with her roles in the latter two period dramas. *The Madwoman of Challot* and *The Trojan Woman* are emblematic of the manner in which Hepburn began appearing in films and plays that went against type. In 1969, she appeared on stage for the first time in years to portray Coco Chanel in *Coco*, and during the next decade, she appeared in an eclectic mix of films, which included a large number of made-for-television movies. In 1973, she starred in the film adaptation of Edward Albee's *A Delicate Balance*, portraying a family matriarch who must deal with an alcoholic sister. That same year, she appeared as Amanda Wingfield in a made-for-television film of Tennessee Williams' *The Glass Menagerie* (1973), a wild role that was the polar opposite of the tranquil character she conveyed at the beginning in *A Delicate Balance*. In arguably the most surprising role of her career, Hepburn then appeared with John Wayne in *Rooster Cogburn*. The grouping of Wayne and Hepburn was seemingly bizarre, as Wayne's right-wing macho sensibility clashed with Hepburn's liberal, progressive sensibility. Although the film itself manages to avoid being especially awkward, the viewers' knowledge of the contrasting star personas of Wayne and Hepburn makes the film a particularly disorienting viewing experience.

Hepburn in *Rooster Cogburn*

Even after reaching the age of 70, Hepburn continued to remain active and received prominent roles. There was little reason for her to retire from a personal standpoint, and she remained in excellent shape, continuing to play tennis and swim on a regular basis. Following *Rooster Cogburn*, she appeared in *Olly Olly Oxen Free*, a comedy in which she plays an eccentric antique shop owner. The most prominent scenes of the film involve Hepburn traveling in a hot air balloon, characteristic of Hepburn's adventurous personality. While many might be unnerved at the prospect, Hepburn treated the experience with adventure and enjoyed the experience.

By the 1980s, Hepburn's physique was starting to fade, and she even had a tremor that affected her movement. Naturally, she planned to work less and less, explaining, "I've had my day - let the kids scramble and sweat it out." Nevertheless, Hepburn appeared in a limited number of films during the decade, most notably *On Golden Pond* (1981) and *Grace Quigley* (1985). *Grace Quigley* was Hepburn's final starring role, featuring her as an old woman who hires a hit man to kill her. Meanwhile, in *On Golden Pond*, she starred with Henry Fonda, continuing a trend that began with *Rooster Cogburn* in which she appeared with aging male stars of the 1940s and 1950s. The sentimental plotline reflects the increasingly conservative nature of the Hepburn persona late in life, as she was relegated to appearing as either a crazy, harmless old woman (as in *Rooster Cogburn*, *Olly Olly Oxen Free*, and *Grace Quigley*) or a simple matriarch (*A Delicate Balance*, *On Golden Pond*). Still, Hepburn retained her vitality and continued to exude the magnetism that had first drawn her to Edwin Knopf decades earlier, even as she relinquished the subversive nature of her characters from the 1930s. She also managed to appear on stage in 1981 in *The West Side Waltz*, and even though she was already in her 70s, critics praised her performance. *New York Times* critic Walter Kerr wrote, "One mysterious thing she has learned to do is breathe unchallengeable life into lifeless lines."

Hepburn with Henry Fonda in *On Golden Pond*

Hepburn's final film appearance was in *Love Affair* (1994), which she had appeared in solely after urging from Warren Beatty, the film's male lead. By this point, her health had already begun deteriorating to the point that acting was very difficult, and the scenes with Hepburn are painful to watch, as her once-athletic frame had become whittled down to a frail shell. Two years after the release of *Love Affair*, she developed pneumonia, which exacerbated her poor health. Around this time, she also began to develop dementia, even though she continued to live and progressed well into her nineties. In 2003, she developed a tumor on her neck, and she died on June 29 of that year.

Chapter 8: Hepburn's Legacy

"Her best films were when she was presented as a woman on her high horse with slightly pretentious, often comically stated ideas about the world. It was for men to bring her down and get her to reveal herself as quite a good gal, sporty and democratic. We liked the idea that aristocratic people would be humanized by democratic values—in her case, by slightly rough-necked and good-natured males." — Film historian and critic Richard Schickel

During the first decade of Katharine Hepburn's film career, the suggestion that she would one day become one of the most beloved figures in American film history would have been laughable. That the public attitude toward Hepburn changed so drastically testifies not only to the diversity of her roles but also to the sheer length of her film and stage careers. Spanning roughly 65 years from beginning to end in 1994, Hepburn outlasted the majority of her contemporaries, and as a result, there were more phases to her career than perhaps any other actress. First, there were her 1930s films, which featured her in subversive, gender-bending roles, with *Christopher Strong* and *Sylvia Scarlett* constituting the most representative examples. After that, she underwent her screwball comedy period, which included both the films with Cary Grant and the early ones with Spencer Tracy. During the 1950s and 1960s, Hepburn entered her spinster period, and finally, in old age, she appeared as either a matriarch or an eccentric old lady. This trajectory coincided with her gradual progression from subversive Hollywood outcast to beloved American icon, a change more drastic than perhaps anyone else's in movie history.

At the same time, some critics have argued that regardless of her fame and reputation, her actual acting skills were overrated. The people making this argument point out that she played characters who resembled what she was like in real life, insinuating that she didn't truly have to act in her roles. This was due in no small part to the fact Hepburn picked some of her parts based on the traits of the characters she was playing, telling a journalist in 1991, "I think I'm always the same. I had a very definite personality and I liked material that showed that personality." But as author David Macaray points out, "Picture Katharine Hepburn in every movie she ever starred in and ask yourself if she's not playing, essentially, the same part over and over...Icon or no icon, let's not confuse a truly fascinating and unique woman with a superior actress." Of course, Hepburn won more Academy Awards (4) than any other actor or actress, and she was nominated 12 times over the span of nearly 50 years. Only Meryl Streep has been nominated more times than Hepburn. It's no surprise that the American Film Institute ranked her the greatest Hollywood legend among all actresses in history.

Regardless of the debate over her acting abilities, there's no question that Hepburn was so different from the norm in real life, and her ability to depict it on the silver screen for millions of viewers helped change the way society viewed women. Film historian Jeanine Basinger noted, "What she brought us was a new kind of heroine—modern and independent. She was beautiful, but she did not rely on that." One writer in the *Los Angeles Times* went so far as to claim, "More than a movie star, Katharine Hepburn was the patron saint of the independent American female."

Hepburn remains one of Hollywood's biggest icons, and the sheer scope of her career makes it difficult to pinpoint all the influences she had on film and culture. Over the course of her career, she displayed a new model for female beauty, one that was almost masculine in its athleticism and angularity, she successfully reconciled an old-money, East Coast/New England sensibility with the populist mores of the Great Depression, she provided an image of the career woman that had previously been unseen in American cinema, and her films displayed the potential for women to occupy a dominant role within the previously patriarchal institution of marriage. Not all of her films displayed each of these themes, but Hepburn's voluminous filmography allowed her to display all the different influences she brought to the table at one time or another. While her films are worth studying in their own right, it is a testament to Hepburn's significance that her legacy manifests through the effects she helped create, all of which are still felt through the representation of women and their roles in both cinema and American culture.

Bibliography

Anderson, Christopher. An Affair to Remember: The Remarkable Love Story of Katharine Hepburn and Spencer Tracy (1997)

Berg, A. Scott. *Kate Remembered*. New York: Berkley, 2003.

Britton, Andrew. *Katharine Hepburn: Star as Feminist*. New York: Columbia University Press, 2003.

Chandler, Charlotte. *I Know Where I'm Going: Katharine Hepburn: A Personal Biography*. New York: Simon & Schuster, 2010.

Curtis, James. Spencer Tracy: A Biography (2011)

Davidson, Bill. Spencer Tracy: Tragic Idol (1988)

Edwards, Ann. *Katharine Hepburn: A Remarkable Woman*. New York: St. Martin's, 2000.

Hepburn, Katharine. *Me*. New York: Random House, 1991.

Hepburn, Katharine. *Katharine Hepburn Once Said…Great Lines to Live By*. New York: HarperCollins, 2003.

Hingham, Charles. *Kate: The Life of Katharine Hepburn*. New York: W.W. Norton & Company, 2004.

Kanin, Garson. Tracy and Hepburn: An Intimate Memoir (2012)

Leaming, Barbara. *Katharine Hepburn*. New York: Proscenium Publishers, Inc., 2000.

Lowe, Brenda. Spencer Tracy Fox Film Actor: The Pre-C0ode Legacy of a Hollywood Legend (2009)

Mann, William J. *Kate: The Woman Who Was Hepburn*. New York: Picador, 2006.

New England Vintage Film Society, Inc. Spencer Tracy, A Life in Pictures (2012)

Porter, Darwin. *Katharine the Great: (1907-1950): Secrets of a Lifetime...Revealed*. New York: Blood Moon Productions, Ltd., 2004.

Swindell, Larry. Spencer Tracy: A Biography (1969)

www.ingramcontent.com/pod-product-compliance
Lightning Source LLC
LaVergne TN
LVHW020514140125
801234LV00020B/397